A User's Guide to
Campaign Finance Reform

A User's Guide to Campaign Finance Reform

Edited by Gerald C. Lubenow

Rowman & Littlefield Publishers, Inc.
Lanham • Boulder • New York • Oxford

Berkeley Public Policy Press
University of California, Berkeley

ROWMAN & LITTLEFIELD PUBLISHERS, INC.

Published in the United States of America
by Rowman & Littlefield Publishers, Inc.
4720 Boston Way, Lanham, Maryland 20706
www.rowmanlittlefield.com

12 Hid's Copse Road, Cumnor Hill, Oxford OX2 9JJ, England

Copyright © 2001 by Rowman & Littlefield Publishers, Inc.

Published under the auspices of Berkeley Public Policy Press.

British Library Cataloguing in Publication Information Available

Library of Congress Cataloging-in-Publication Data Available

ISBN 0-7425-1794-2 (cloth : alk. paper)
ISBN 0-7425-1795-0 (pbk. : alk. paper)

Printed in the United States of America

⊖™ The paper used in this publication meets the minimum requirements of American National Standard for Information Sciences—Permanence of Paper for Printed Library Materials, ANSI/NISO Z39.48-1992.

Contents

Preface

In the forest of campaign finance, the reformers and the press are hedgehogs; the political scientists are foxes. The reference comes from a fragment of Greek poetry by Archilochus: "The fox knows many things, but the hedgehog knows one big thing." Its meaning was plumbed most famously by Isaiah Berlin in his essay "The Hedgehog and the Fox." Among thinkers and writers, and, perhaps among human beings in general, he wrote, there exists a great chasm between the hedgehogs who relate everything to a single, universal organizing principle, and the foxes who pursue many ends, often unrelated and contradictory. When it comes to campaign finance, the hedgehogs in the reform movement and the media are driven by a singular vision: politics in the United States is corrupt and the reason is money. Reduce the role of money, and politicians will be free to ignore the special interests and focus on the public interest.

The academic foxes who view politics through the lens of social science see a much different picture. Money is a major factor in politics, to be sure. But so are parties and constituents and issues and interest groups and regional alliances and ideological factions and gender and ethnicity, and a host of factors, any one of which can play an important role depending on the issue and the circumstances.

Research findings on campaign finance are diverse and often contradictory. Political scientists disagree about the role of money. But few political scientists would argue that money trumps all. Many would disagree with reformers that if money could be removed from the political equation we would experience some sort of public interest policy nirvana. Indeed, some would even argue that the problem is not that there is too much money in politics but that there is too little.

As a result of years of research, the academic foxes do know many things. For example, contrary to reformist claims that political participation is declining because voters are turned off by the amount of money in politics, studies show that people who are satisfied with the political system participate and abstain in roughly the same proportions as those who are dissatisfied. They know that despite claims of overwhelming public demand for reform, poll after poll shows that campaign finance ranks far down the list of voters concerns. As for the charges of corruption, historians can easily point to past practices that make the current system seem positively pristine.

To get an overview of the current state of research on campaign finance, we assembled a group of the nation's leading scholars at the Institute of Governmental Studies for an intensive two-day assessment of the current research and the major questions that would benefit from further study. As a follow-up, we asked several of the participants to write chapters that we could publish as a guide for scholars, practitioners, and the public.

This book is the result. Its aim is to help readers understand how the current political finance system works. The scholars have different points of view and draw different conclusions. The one thing they would all agree on is that reform should flow from an understanding not only of the strengths and weaknesses of the current system, but from a careful examination of the potential problems that may arise as the result of reform.

Having sailed easily through the Senate, campaign finance reform encountered rougher waters in the House. And the opposition came not just from conservative Republicans. There was growing opposition among minority legislators, many of whom count on party soft money to fuel their campaigns. It turns out that soft money for voter registration and get-out-the-vote efforts is especially important to support shy minority candidates.

Early on, as many as 37 House Democrats indicated they might oppose the Senate bill. Their complaints focused on amendments to McCain-Feingold that would double the allowable hard money contribution and triple the aggregate amount an individual can give.

A User's Guide to Campaign Finance Reform raises a number of other interesting questions about McCain-Feingold; some of them have to do with the assumptions about the current system on which the proposed reforms are based, others with the likely impact on the system should the reforms pass. The top experts assembled for the Berkeley conference represented, as the book does, a broad spectrum of academic opinion on reform, all of it based on the latest research. That opinion often diverged quite sharply from the positions taken by special interest groups like Common Cause that are devoted to the cause of reform. As Norman Ornstein of the American Enterprise Institute observes in his essay, "The political science community has done its own extensive research on campaigns and campaign financing, but for most of the post-1974 period, its work was largely ignored by reporters, interest groups, and politicians alike, especially when it contradicted their own assumptions and assertions." Ornstein has been meeting with a group of scholars since 1996 to discuss realistic goals of meaningful campaign reform. After weighing the political problems inherent in reform, he is convinced that constructive reform with wide bipartisan support is in fact possible. To help define what it might look like, he has written "Eight Modest Ideas for Meaningful Campaign Finance Reform."

Not only have reformers generally ignored scholarly findings in the past, they are now focused on an area of campaign finance about which no one knows much for certain. "We know relatively little about how political parties raise and spend soft money," observes UC Berkeley's Ray La Raja whose research focuses on soft money and whose chapter addresses those questions in detail. Data on soft money, he notes, have only been available in the past few election cycles, and there are just a handful of scholarly studies of party activity with soft money.

While reformers claim that soft money is used largely to buy attack ads, La Raja's research shows the parties spent as much on direct mobilization and grassroots efforts as they did on ads. His findings suggest that soft money encourages party building and party integration, much as Congress desired. To reduce the potential for corruption, he recommends that Congress cap soft money but not ban it.

"A robust debate on campaign finance should consider a range of political values before coming to judgment about the merits of proposed reforms," argues La Raja. "As far as soft money goes, our collective knowledge is minimal, even though the nation's lawmakers are on the threshold of passing reforms that would eliminate this source of party funds. To paraphrase Winston Churchill on the RAF, rarely have so many sought such far-reaching reform on the basis of so little knowledge."

We hope the *User's Guide* will help close this gap and move the debate beyond the current rote denunciations of alleged corruption in the current system. In the book's opening essay, historian Robert Mutch shows that special interests and money have been integral to American politics since the days of George Washington.

Ken Mayer of the University of Wisconsin offers a devastating critique of press coverage: "Inadequate media coverage of campaign finance issues and the simplistic arguments offered by many campaign finance reformers make it impossible to distinguish true corruption from the every-day pull and haul of politics. Too often, reform arguments reduce complicated political processes to a simplistic money-equals-votes relationship. In so doing, they construct explanations that fail to meet basic logical standards. The strategy is more rhetorical than logical and usually involves some variant of the following flawed syllogism:

Major Premise: Interest groups lobby and contribute money to Congress
Minor Premise: Congress makes legislative decisions

Conclusion: All legislative decisions are based solely on interest group contributions and lobbying
This argument leads naturally to the conclusion that *everything* about political decision-making is corrupt and crowds out arguments about the merits and flaws of particular legislative proposals."

Making an argument they concede "is heretical, especially for three Democrats," Steve Ansolabehere of MIT and his co-authors Alan Gerber and James M. Snyder, Jr., find that, contrary to the claims of reformers and the media, campaign spending has not exploded in recent years. They argue that the Gross Domestic Product rather than the Consumer Price Index should be used to normalize campaign spending over time. By that standard, they write, "It is clear that campaign spending has not grown faster than the nation's income. Total campaign spending in presidential years hovers around one-hundredth of one percent of Gross Domestic Product." This relationship, they note, has held relatively steady since 1912.

Turning to arguments made by reformers and trumpeted by the press that special interests benefit enormously from the campaign finance system, Ansolabehere and his colleagues conclude: "To put the matter bluntly, the criticism doesn't add up to much." Corruption generated by campaign contributions, they note, is no worse today than it was 25 years ago, "and it may have even lessened over the last two decades. . . . This fact turns the rhetoric of reformers on its head."

Northeastern University's Bill Mayer took an exhaustive look at the polling data on campaign finance and found, "Despite the efforts of reformers to create the impression of a mandate for change, most Americans, whatever their preferences as to specific reforms, don't seem very concerned about campaign finance and are skeptical about the political prospects of reform and its likely consequences . . . I was, frankly, surprised how strong the evidence is on this point."

Clyde Wilcox of Georgetown examined the role of contributions as a form of political participation and found soft money donors had significantly more access to politicians than the average voter. "If soft money donors are especially unrepresentative," he writes, "and if they have even greater access, then a ban or limit on soft money would curb some of the most egregious aspects of participatory distortion." But, while Congress ponders limits on political giving, he suggests they might also think about ways to encourage more voters to donate to political campaigns. "Whatever reforms may finally pass," he notes, "it will be important to chart their impact on individual donors as well as on the financial health of parties and interest groups."

Examining the increasing role played by the courts in the area of campaign finance, Joshua Rosenkranz, of The Brennan Center at New York University offers some preliminary thoughts on areas political scientists could explore if they wish to have more of an influence on judicial decisions. He reviews the current legal framework of campaign finance doctrine, set by *Buckley v. Valeo,* and then turns to some of *Buckley*'s basic premises that have never been subjected to rigorous assessment by the political science community. He then summarizes some of the current legal controversies—from the regulation of sham issue advocacy to soft money to contribution limits to public financing—and describes the key legal issues and the empirical questions that could help the courts resolve them. "My hope," he writes, "is to encourage political science research into campaign finance questions that are sure to confound the courts, so that political scientists will secure their rightful place as active participants in the formulation of constitutional principles, rather than relegating themselves to the role of mystified and incensed reporters of botched judicial forays into the political thicket."

As I noted earlier, *A User's Guide to Campaign Finance Reform* grew out of a gathering sponsored by the Institute of Governmental Studies and the Citizens' Research Foundation on the campus of the University of California, Berkeley in the summer of 2000. We would like to thank the Carnegie Corporation of New York and the Steven and Michele Kirsch Foundation of Silicon Valley for their generous support of that conference and this book.

Gerald C. Lubenow
University of California, Berkeley
June 2001

Chapter 1

Three Centuries of Campaign Finance Law

Robert E. Mutch

In 1699, members of the Virginia House of Burgesses asked themselves the same questions that define today's campaign finance debate: How should we regulate campaign money? Why should we regulate it at all? The record of this early debate is very sketchy so we don't know how the legislators answered these questions. What we do know is that they enacted what may have been the first campaign finance law on this side of the Atlantic: a prohibition against the bribery of voters. This prohibition was typical of American campaign finance laws for the next 200 years. These laws were concerned almost exclusively with what came to be known as "corrupt practices," i.e., the manipulation of votes through bribery, intimidation, and fraud. These laws reflected almost universal agreement on the answer to the "why" question. The purpose of campaign finance regulation was to protect the integrity of elections.

Consensus on this traditional concern was eroded by the industrial revolution. In response to political machines, the rise of large industrial corporations, and the widening disparity of wealth that occurred after the Civil War, campaign finance regulation became campaign finance reform. By the 20th century, reformers had begun to see campaign finance law as a way to address the larger, and far more contentious, issue of the proper relationship between money and political power. This expansion from a focus on procedural issues to matters of democratic theory explains the ideological intensity of today's debate. And though today's debate is fundamentally different from those of earlier centuries,

1

the central concern remains the same: corruption. The continuity is more apparent than real, however, because there is no longer any agreement on what corruption means or how serious a problem it is.

This lack of clarity is apparent in another feature of the current debate, the historical arguments that both sides are beginning to use to buttress their opposing views on the proper role of wealth in a democracy. These arguments shed some light on how campaign finance law has changed over the centuries and why the debate over it has become so tangled.

The Current Debate

It must be admitted at the outset that "argument" probably is too grand a term. Without citing anyone in particular, on either side, what I'm referring to are for the most part no more than assumptions, often unstated ones, or throwaway references to what is taken to be common knowledge. For example, implicit in the arguments of many reformers is the assumption that big money in politics is a relatively recent development, meaning any time in the last 100 years or so. In their view, money represents a new threat to our democracy, one that should be addressed with laws to limit the political power of wealth.

Reform opponents, on the other hand, assume there has been money in elections for as long as there have been elections. These opponents may not be of one mind about money—some see it as a positive good, others as a necessary evil—but all agree that attempts to reduce its role are at best futile and at worst dangerous. In fact, they tend to claim that the greatest threat to democracy lies in the reform laws themselves.

Because reformers see big money in politics as a relatively recent phenomenon, they also assume that the political power of wealth has never been greater than it is now. To them, this means that corruption is a bigger problem now than it has ever been. Not so, say reform opponents. In the past, they point out, political money came from only a handful of sources. The broader base of campaign fundraising today means that corruption is less of a problem now than at any time in our history. Both sides might agree, albeit for different reasons, that campaign finance reform has been a labor of Sisyphus. Since the end of the 19th century, reformers have launched several efforts to enact laws reducing the political power of wealth. Each time they had to start afresh at the bottom of the hill when the laws failed to achieve that end. To reformers this pattern must seem like a torment inflicted on them by the vengeful gods of Greek mythology; their opponents are more likely to see it as the inevitable result of the reformers' own delusions.

But if there has always been big money in politics, why did reformers start pushing their rock up the hill only toward the end of the 19th century? And if corruption is no longer a serious problem, why don't reformers just walk away from the rock and declare victory? Behind these questions and the arguments reviewed above is the persistent historical question, How did we get here? Which itself is but another way of asking, Where are we? If, as reform opponents say, we are here because this is, in a sense, where we always have been, then why are we having this debate at all? Or has the debate, too, always been with us?

Five Questions

We can begin to answer these big questions only by going back into our history and asking a series of smaller ones:

1. What kinds of campaign finance laws were on the books or under debate?
2. How widespread were the practices these laws addressed?
3. Why were the laws passed, i.e., in response to what kinds of events?
4. Did the laws work as intended? Why or why not?
5. What ideas of good government motivated the laws' supporters and opponents?

These questions will be asked of two periods in our history. The first is Virginia in the 1750s, focusing on the campaign practices George Washington used in his first election to public office and the laws that then regulated campaign finance. The second is the 1880s, which gave us the first presidential campaign finance scandal in 1888 and the beginning of the scandal-reform cycle.

Gentleman Freeholders

In 1758, George Washington won his first election to public office: a seat in the Virginia House of Burgesses, the lower house of the colonial legislature, from the frontier county of Frederick. Although he lived at his Fairfax County estate, Mt. Vernon, under Virginia law he was eligible to stand for office in Frederick because he also owned a plantation there.

There is a small but noticeable surge of interest in this election among campaign finance scholars. This new interest centers on the one recorded expense of Washington's 1758 campaign: £39 for beer, wine, and liquor to dispense to the voters on election day.[1]

According to Sydnor, £39 was a large sum for the time, "several times more than enough to buy the house and land of the voter who barely met the minimum

---

[1]William Wright Abbott, ed., *The Papers of George Washington, Colonial Series* (Charlottesville: University Press of Virginia, 1983–), 5: 331–34.

franchise requirements."[2] This expenditure is attracting attention today because it appears to be an instance in which money played as direct a role in an 18th-century election as it does in those of our own day; and because that money was spent on a practice, called treating, that has been considered a corrupt practice since the 19th century.

Historian Gil Troy, for example, cited Washington's 1758 campaign to make the point that "currying the people's favor has always been costly" and that attempts to reform campaign financing are likely to be futile. But the Center for Responsive Politics also mentioned it in a 1995 pamphlet because "reformers need to know what they're up against—in this case, a 200-year tradition in which . . . private money has always been the medium of political democracy."[3] They may be on opposite sides of the current debate, but they agree on one thing: The way George Washington financed his campaign 250 years ago is relevant today. It is that assumption that will be examined here.

What Campaign Finance Laws Were in Effect in Virginia in 1758?

There were two. The first, enacted in 1699 and amended twice by the time George Washington became a candidate, prohibited the bribing of voters. Its core provision read: "[N]o person or persons hereafter to be elected to serve in the General Assembly . . . shall . . . directly or indirectly, give, present, or allow to any person or persons having voice or vote in such election any money, meat, drink, entertainment, or provision . . . in order to be elected."[4]

The second law addressed a more circuitous means of inflating a candidate's vote. Some candidates and their supporters were not above transferring title to parts of their land just long enough to qualify men who would vote for them. To uphold "the rights of the true freeholders," the Virginia General Assembly passed "An Act to declare who shall have a right to vote in the Election of Burgesses . . . and for preventing fraudulent Conveiances, in order to multiply Votes." The 1736 law denied the vote to those who had not owned the required

---

[2]Charles S. Sydnor, *American Revolutionaries in the Making: Political Practices in Washington's Virginia* (New York: Free Press, 1952).

[3]Gil Troy, "Money and Politics: The Oldest Connection," *The Wilson Quarterly* 21 (1997): 16; Committee for Responsive Politics (CRP), *A Brief History of Money in Politics* (Washington, D.C.: Center for Responsive Politics, 1995), 5. Bradley A. Smith also mentions this election, but gets the historical context right (*Unfree Speech: The Folly of Campaign Finance Reform* [Princeton: Princeton University Press, 2001], 18).

[4]William W. Hening, *The Statutes at Large: Being a Collection of all the Laws of Virginia from the First Session of the Legislature in the Year 1619*, 13 vols. (Philadelphia and Richmond, 1819–1823), vol. III, 243.

amount of property—25 acres of improved, or 100 acres of unimproved, land—for at least one year.[5]

How Widespread Were the Practices These Laws Addressed?

Bribery of Voters

It's not possible to determine how prevalent bribery at the polls was in 18th-century Virginia. Unlike so many of the problems in the history of campaign finance, though, this is not one of insufficient data. Rather, it is that we cannot today distinguish between behavior that was illegal and behavior that was customary, rooted in now unfamiliar political traditions. Washington's election-day expenditure, for example, at first appears to be just what the 1699 law prohibited. Yet the candidate he defeated did not complain, and for what was then good reason. "Treating was not simply a way of buying support. The paternalistic dominance of the gentry was expressed in their acceptance of an obligation to show 'liberality' toward their poorer neighbors. The candidates confirmed their character as magnanimous gentlemen when they stood treat to all voters, regardless of how they voted."[6] Nor was this practice confined to Virginia. "In the southern colonies, election time was an occasion for eating, drinking, and being merry at the expense of the candidates, who acted the role of genial hosts of county or parish freeholders. It was as much a social as a political occasion, at least for the voter."[7]

That Washington saw himself in the role of magnanimous gentleman rather than corrupter of the electorate is clear from a letter to one of his chief supporters: "I hope no Exception were taken to any that voted against me but that all were alike treated and all had enough; it is what I much desir'd—my only fear is that you spent with too sparing a hand."[8] According to the most thorough study yet of 18th-century political practices, treating voters with strong drink was a common if not universal practice.[9]

It was also a practice that could deteriorate into blunter appeals for support. Defeated candidates who believed their opponents owed their victories to bribery could bring charges before the House by submitting "undue election" petitions. In the 20 years preceding Washington's 1758 election, the House decided

---

[5]*Ibid.*, vol. IV, 475–76.

[6]Rhys Isaac, *The Transformation of Virginia, 1740–1790* (Chapel Hill: University of North Carolina Press, 1982), 113.

[7]Chilton Williamson, *American Suffrage from Property to Democracy, 1760–1860* (Princeton: Princeton University Press, 1960), 56.

[8]Abbott, *Washington Papers*, 5: 349.

[9]John G. Kolp, "The Flame of Burgessing: Elections and the Political Communities of Colonial Virginia, 1728–1775, Ph.D. dissertation, University of Iowa, 1988, 52.

16 disputed election cases, at least seven of which involved charges that in en-
tertaining voters the successful candidates had stepped over the line and
committed bribery. The disposal of these cases suggests that drawing this line
was difficult even then.[10]

Candidates or their supporters were found to have bribed voters in only two
of the seven cases. These cases were not decided easily. The usual procedure for
handling undue election petitions was to send them first to the House Privileges
and Elections Committee. After hearing testimony, the Committee sent its rec-
ommendations to the entire House for a floor vote. In four of the cases, the
committee found the elections had been achieved by illegal means and recom-
mended unseating the winners. But the entire House rejected the committee's
finding in two of those cases. In another case, the House decided there had been
wrongdoing where the committee had found none.

The spending by which one candidate courted the voters in a manner sanc-
tioned by long tradition looked very much like the spending by which another
candidate tried to undermine both law and custom. This is why it is so difficult
now to distinguish the spending the House of Burgesses found acceptable from
the spending that led it to grant undue election petitions and unseat one of its
members.

Fraudulent Freeholds

There is even less evidence for this practice. Of the 16 elections whose outcomes were disputed between 1738 and 1758, not one involved the creation of
fraudulent freeholds.

Although there is little evidence one way or the other, it is likely that both
practices were rare. One factor that would have kept them down was the small
size of 18th-century Virginia electorates. At a time when citizens had to meet a
property qualification to vote, between one-half and three-fourths of free, white,
adult males owned no land at all.[11] These electorates appear to have been small
enough so that candidates and their gentry supporters could very well know
most voters by name.

Because it would have been very difficult in such small societies to conceal
attempts to bribe voters or manufacture freeholders, it's reasonable to assume
that such attempts would have been made only in very close elections. But close
races, too, were rare. In fact, most 18th-century elections do not seem to have
been contests at all. "[C]ompetition in House of Burgesses elections occurred in

---

[10]The seven cases were for Accomack County, Gloucester County, Richmond
County, Prince George and Hanover counties, Elizabeth City County, and Lunenburg
County.

[11]Thomas Jefferson, *Notes on the State of Virginia* (New York: Harper & Row,
1964), 112; Jackson Turner Main, "The Distribution of Property in Post-Revolutionary
Virginia," *Mississippi Valley Historical Review* 41 (1954): 243.

only one-third of the documented elections between 1728 and 1775. In the remaining two-thirds, no real contest took place, and the freeholders . . . at most were simply asked to affirm the candidates running unopposed."[12]

The primary reason for believing these practices to have been rare is that it was unnecessary. The planter gentry had other, legal, ways to use their economic power to influence the votes of small freeholders. The gentry's political dominance stemmed not only from their ownership of half the land in that agricultural economy but also from their control over extension of credit to smaller tobacco planters.[13] "[T]he combined power of [gentlemen's] public personae and their ability to wield influence—to dispense patronage or reward one set of interests at the expense of another—guaranteed them the suffrages of less prominent neighbors."[14]

Once having gained the gentry backing necessary to be regarded as a serious contender for office, candidates normally could secure the compliance of freeholders without being heavy handed. "[P]owerful men would let their friends, relatives, and dependents know how they stood toward the candidates. Thus, elections often were settled before they were held."[15] When election day did come, a candidate's supporters continued to exert their influence simply by being the first to vote. Because voting was oral, the early and public votes of wealthy and powerful men "turned to that candidate the votes of lesser men who respected their judgment or were obligated to them."[16] Not all candidates relied on these traditional, indirect methods. Some were reported to have threatened their debtors and at least one carried out that threat by foreclosing on 33 debtors who had voted against him.[17]

The first to cast a vote for George Washington in 1758 was Thomas Lord Fairfax, the largest landowner in Virginia. Immediately following him were the rector of Frederick Parish, the principal clergyman of the Established Church in the county; the founder and leading citizen of Winchester, the county seat; more large Frederick County landowners; and a string of rich merchants from Alexandria and Falmouth. When he stood for reelection in Frederick in 1761, Wash-

[12]John G. Kolp, "The Dynamics of Electoral Competition in Pre-Revolutionary Virginia," *William and Mary Quarterly* 3rd ser., 49 (1992): 670.

[13]Isaac, *Transformation*, 133.

[14]Richard R. Beeman, "Deference, Republicanism, and the Emergence of Popular Politics in Eighteenth-Century America," *William and Mary Quarterly* 3rd ser., 49 (1992): 401–30.

[15]Sydnor, *American Revolutionaries*, 52.

[16]Isaac, *Transformation*, 67.

[17]T. E. Campbell, *Colonial Caroline: A History of Caroline County, Virginia* (Richmond, Va.: The Dietz Press, 1954), 86–87.

ington let the county sheriff know that "it might be an advantage" if his friends "could . . . be hurried in at the first of the Poll."[18]

Why Were the Laws Passed?

Bribery of Voters

Recent English law may have been the inspiration here. The House of Burgesses passed the prohibition against bribery of voters in response to a 1699 petition "from Accomack County praying That a Law may be made agreeable to the Statutes of England to prevent the undue Election of Burgesses."[19] The English law referred to was passed in 1696, after decades in which increased competition for seats in Parliament had raised both the cost of elections and the incidence of bribery.[20]

It's worth noting a failed attempt to strengthen the 1699 law. In 1752, after the House rejected charges of bribery in a Prince George County election, three leading members of the House drafted a bill "to prevent the giving, or selling, strong Liquor on any Election-Day, before the Election shall be over." Unlike existing laws, which prohibited actions generally agreed to be corrupt, this law would have restricted a traditional campaign activity on the ground that it might be used for corrupt purposes. The House rejected the bill.[21]

Fraudulent Freeholds

A complaint from the speaker of the House gave rise to this law. The speaker charged the sheriff of York County with having "made several Leases of small Parcels of Land, of little or no Value, on Purpose to qualify Persons to vote" in a 1736 election.[22] The sheriff admitted he had done this, and that "he expected the Lessees would vote for those Persons whom he should like, at the said Election, otherwise he should not have made the Leases."[23]

The House reprimanded the sheriff, resolving that he had "acted corruptly, against Law, and the Duty of his Office."[24] In saying the sheriff had acted

---

[18]Abbott, *Washington Papers*, 7: 43.

[19]H. R. McIlwaine, *Journals of the House of Burgesses of Virginia, 1619–1776* (Richmond, Va.: The Colonial Press, E. Waddey Co.) 12 vols., 1699, 150.

[20]Cornelius O'Leary, *The Elimination of Corrupt Practices in British Elections, 1868–1911* (Harmondsworth: Penguin Books Ltd., 1967), 18; J. H. Plumb, *The Growth of Political Stability in England, 1675–1725* (Harmondsworth: Penguin Books, 1967), 53, 144–45.

[21]H. R. McIlwaine, *House Journals* 1752–55, 51, 56, 64, 70–71.

[22]*Ibid.*, 1736, 276.

[23]*Ibid.*, 283.

[24]*Ibid.*, 282–83.

against the law, the House clearly did not mean he had violated a statute. No such statute existed and the House immediately ordered the Privileges and Elections Committee to prepare a bill that would create one. Within three weeks, a bill "declaring who shall have a Right to vote at Elections" had been passed by the House and the Council and been signed into law by the governor.

Did the Laws Work as Intended?

It's unlikely that either of the prohibited practices would have played more than a very minor part in the electoral politics of mid-18th-century Virginia even without the two laws. But any restraining effect those laws did have probably is best explained by the fact that they were self-imposed. In both cases, the House of Burgesses acted on complaints not from a critical public but from within the gentry class itself. The laws were the means by which the planter gentry regulated its own behavior, and self-imposed restrictions tend to work better than those imposed from without.

What Ideas Motivated the Laws' Supporters and Opponents?

There were disagreements over the bribery and the fraudulent freehold laws —both were compromises that came out of House-Council conference committees—but there is no evidence that mid-18th-century Virginia was engaged in anything like today's philosophical debate over campaign finance law. Rather, both laws furthered a common idea of good government that was centuries old.

When George Washington stood for office in 1758, the 40-shilling freehold law had been in effect for 300 years.[25] Montesquieu explained why only property owners should vote: "[A]ll citizens . . . should have the right to vote except those whose estate is so humble that they are deemed to have no will of their own."[26] In this context we can understand why the House of Burgesses accused the York County sheriff of acting "corruptly, against Law" by leasing small plots of land to create freeholders who would vote as he wished. In a society in which nearly everyone was in some way dependent upon someone else (including Washington himself, whose political career owed a great deal to the patronage of Lord Fairfax), it was important that political loyalties grew "naturally" out of economic and social ties. The gentry's "constant struggle for prestige and supremacy" played as large a role in Virginia politics as in that of England, where "a county election furnished an opportunity . . . of testing the social stand-

---

[25]O'Leary, *Elimination of Corrupt Practices*, 6.

[26]Montesquieu, *The Spirit of the Laws* (Cambridge: Cambridge University Press, 1989), 160.

ing of an individual."[27] The sheriff's short-lived gain in political power owed little to his social standing and was therefore seen as corrupt.

Treating was almost as ancient as the freehold law. It was first reported in 1467 and by the 17th century, "it was the custom to entertain the freeholders at an election" in many English counties.[28] In England, too, the line between bribery and *noblesse oblige* was difficult to draw. "Whether an offer of money or some other advantage was to be held as corrupt was determined entirely by circumstances. Hence the severe penalties inflicted on a few for offenses not materially different from those to which many members owed their seats."[29]

Treating was an integral part of political systems dominated by aristocracies, systems in which a candidate "had to show due regard to his constituents . . . and in short be 'indefatigable in serving his friends.'"[30] Let those same aristocrats bribe voters, though, and they begin to weaken the legitimacy of gentry rule by undermining the integrity of the elections on which it is based. The line between magnanimous gentleman and corrupter of the electorate may have been hard to draw in particular cases, but freeholders of all ranks knew that there had to be such a line.

Today, only historians can distinguish between the two practices. That the average citizen today sees Washington's election-day expenditure as embarrassing or titillating indicates that the accepted political ideas of his time are now so foreign that we no longer know what to make of them. In some ways, 18th-century politics can be seen as the beginnings of our own. In other ways, it can be seen as the last expression of a kind of politics that dates back to the Roman republic but which has long since vanished. In republican Rome, which also combined laws against bribing voters with a tradition of treating them, "a noble could traditionally extend a limited amount of hospitality . . . during the course of his election campaign without falling foul of the laws on corruption.[31] Cicero, himself the author of an antibribery law, once argued on behalf of a client charged with violating it, "I cannot see why candidates for official posts should be prevented from performing acts of kindness, which are products of generosity, not of bribery."[32]

---

[27] J. E. Neale, *The Elizabethan House of Commons* (Harmondsworth: Penguin Books, 1949), 24–25.

[28] *Ibid.,* 66.

[29] O'Leary, *Elimination of Corrupt Practices,* 12.

[30] Sir Lewis Namier, *The Structure of Politics at the Accession of George III* (London: Macmillan and Co., 1965), 161.

[31] E. S. Staveley, *Greek and Roman Voting and Elections* (Ithaca: Cornell University Press, 1972), 197.

[32] Cicero, *On Government* (London: Penguin Books, 1993), 152.

Making Politics Pay

The Gilded Age, on the other hand, looks very familiar. By the 1880s, we find many of the elements that still characterize politics at the beginning of the 21st century: huge campaign contributions from business corporations, citizens groups and labor unions clamoring for political reform, and a vigorous public debate over what constitutes good government. The professionalization of politics and the industrialization of the economy were well under way, especially in the North. The merchant elites and landed gentry that had provided the leaders of the colonial and early national eras were still influential and continued sending their members into the upper ranks of government. But the days of their political and economic supremacy were over.

The transition from the classical republican model of small electorates and aristocratic leadership to a mass democracy led by professional politicians meant the end of an electoral system in which candidates paid their own campaign expenses. Carl Russell Fish, one of the first historians of the civil service, put it this way: "It is an essential idea of democracy that those leaders . . . must not be gentlemen of wealth and leisure, but they must . . . belong to the class that makes its own living. If, then, they are to devote their time to politics, politics must be made to pay."[33]

How do we make politics pay and how do we pay for our politics? These problems—which the standard texts of democratic theory do not address and which still are unresolved—first arose in the 19th century.

What Campaign Finance Laws Were in Effect in the Gilded Age?

There were two: the Pendleton Act, the federal civil service reform law enacted in 1883; and the Australian ballot laws, reforms that made the ballot both official and secret, which states began enacting in 1888.

Pendleton Act

As a campaign finance measure—and civil service reform never was aimed solely at ending a system of political funding—the Pendleton Act sought to end the practice of funding political parties through assessments on the salaries of government employees. The act created a class of government employees who not only had to win office through competitive examination rather than political preference, but who were exempted from political assessments. The Pendleton Act was not the first law to address political assessments. The first known cases of assessments were those the Democratic party levied on U.S. customs employ-

---

[33]Carl Russell Fish, *The Civil Service and the Patronage* (Cambridge, Mass.: Harvard University Press, 1920), 156.

ees in New York City during the 1830s. An 1839 House report of "regular taxation of public officers . . . for the support of party elections" at the New York customs house led to a Whig bill to prohibit all federal officers from making campaign contributions. The bill did not pass.[34]

A much narrower bill did pass in 1867. In that year, Congress inserted into a navy appropriations bill a prohibition against the solicitation of political contributions from workers in U.S. Navy yards. This oddly selective provision arose out of a factional conflict within the Republican party, between President Andrew Johnson, who technically had appointed the navy yard workers, and the Radicals, who controlled Congress. The radicals acted after reports of attempts to form "Johnson parties" at navy yards in Philadelphia and New York.[35]

Nine years later, just before the closely contested presidential election of 1876, the Democrats managed to pass a broader, but equally partisan, measure. In a futile attempt to prevent the GOP from using their control of the executive branch to raise money for Rutherford B. Hayes' campaign, the Democratic majority of the House inserted a prohibition against political assessments into a general appropriations bill. Almost one year later, President Hayes backed up this law with an executive order that "No assessments for political purposes . . . should be allowed."[36]

Australian Ballot

The ballot reform movement did focus on campaign financing in that its primary aim was to reduce campaign spending and stop the bribery and intimidation of voters. E. L. Godkin, editor of *The Nation* and the best-known reformer of the period, put the argument succinctly: "[A] secret ballot is the surest as well as the simplest remedy for bribery at the polls."[37] Most states already used what was called simply "the ballot." In the decades after Independence, most of the new states rejected the British system of open, oral voting and allowed voters to write the names of their chosen candidates on pieces of paper or, later, printed ballots. This system seems to have been sufficient to provide secrecy and a barrier to bribery at least into the 1830s.[38] By the 1880s, it was clear that further measures were necessary.

---

[34]Robert E. Mutch, *Campaigns, Congress, and Courts: The Making of Federal Campaign Finance Law* (New York: Praeger, 1988), xvi.

[35]See the House and Senate debates in the *Congressional Globe*, 39th Cong., 2nd Sess., Feb. 27 and March 1, 1867.

[36]U.S. Senate, *Senate Report 427:* 1.

[37]E. L. Godkin, editorial, *The Nation*, Nov. 22, 1888, 406.

[38]For voting procedures in Boston and New York in the 1820s and early 1830s, see the testimony in Great Britain House of Commons, *Sessional Papers* vol. 8, "Report from the Select Committee on Bribery at Elections" (August 1835). Descriptions of American

By the 1870s, the political parties had taken over the job of providing ballots to voters. The cost of printing these ballots—which listed only a party's own candidates—and paying thousands of party workers to distribute them at polling places probably made up the great majority of election expenses in the years before ballot reform laws. Because each party's ballots were of a distinctive size and color, it was easy for party poll watchers to see how people voted even where polling booths were provided. State adoption of the Australian ballot law—so named because it originated in that country—made the ballot secret by making its printing and distribution a state responsibility. Under the reform laws, state governments printed "blanket" ballots that listed the candidates of all parties. Once all voters were given the same official ballot to take into the polling booth, it became far more difficult for poll watchers to determine how each person voted. With the adoption of this reform, states removed the greater part of the parties' campaign costs and reduced the bribery of voters.

The first disclosure laws, seen as a second line of defense against the bribery of voters, were enacted as amendments to state Australian ballot laws. These "publicity" laws required the reporting of expenditures in an attempt to prevent candidates and parties from using money illegally. Reformers began calling for such laws soon after the 1888 election. Seeing that ballot reform was beginning to sweep the country, *The Nation* said "the next step in reform" should be "a comprehensive law limiting the expenditures of candidates and requiring a sworn statement of all such expenditures after election."[39] These laws, which were easy to evade, did not catch on in the same way ballot reform had done. By the end of the century, only 18 states had enacted disclosure requirements, three of which had already repealed them. Disclosure did not become a permanent part of most states' laws until the wave of campaign finance reform that followed the 1905 revelations of corporate financing for Theodore Roosevelt's presidential campaign of the previous year. By that time, the purpose of disclosure had changed and was seen more as a way of discovering where the money was coming from than where it went.[40]

How Widespread Were the Practices These Laws Addressed?

Political Assessments

Assessments on the salaries of government employees probably were the largest single source of financing for election campaigns in the late 19th century. In addition to the expected assessments by congressional campaign committees,

---

voting were given by Joseph Parkes, Alexis deTocqueville, Henry Van Wart, Samuel Aspinwall Goddard, and George Ticknor.

[39]E. L. Godkin, editorial, *The Nation,* January 24, 1889.

[40]Mutch, *Campaigns, Congress, and Courts,* 1–29.

many federal government employees had to pay additional sums to state party committees. In the 1860s, 1870s, and early 1880s—years in which the civil service more than doubled in size and in which the Republican party exercised unbroken control of the White House—"the money collected by Republican congressional committees came largely from employees of the United States government."[41] In 1879–1880, the Democrats took advantage of their rare good fortune in having won a majority of seats in the Senate by creating a select committee to inquire into GOP methods of marshalling economic support for their campaigns. The committee reported that Republicans had levied a two percent assessment on federal civil servants in 1876, and had raised 88 percent of its 1878 campaign funds from one percent assessments on those same employees. Democrats raised less than one-twentieth of that amount in 1878, all from members of Congress and private donors.[42]

The Democrats professed shock at the very idea of such fundraising, arguing that the collection of campaign funds "from persons in the public service . . . is contrary to the spirit of our governmental institutions and in direct antagonism to freedom of choice by the people."[43] In their minority report, the Republicans protested that all money collected in response to their solicitation letters had been contributed voluntarily and so should not be called assessments at all. They pointed out that the committee had "not been able to show that any pressure was made on the employees."[44] Although the Democrats had only a fraction of the GOP's federal patronage power, they "assessed wherever and whenever they were able."[45]

Bribery and Intimidation of Voters

We will never know just how frequently or how many elections were "debauched," to use the reformers' term. It's likely that reformers of the time were prone to exaggerate the extent of election-day abuses. Nonetheless, it does appear that the buying and selling of votes was practiced on a large scale in the 1880s. The 1888 presidential election produced the notorious "blocks of five" letter. This was a letter from the Republican National Committee advising the Indiana GOP to organize "floaters," i.e., those who sold their votes, into blocks of five, each under the watchful eye of a party worker. That party worker was responsible for seeing that all five men showed up at the polls and voted as promised. According to at least one contemporary observer, this practice was not unusual: "If the number of 'floaters' . . . is relatively large to the number of

---

[41] Louise Overacker, *Money in Elections* (New York: Macmillan, 1932), 103.

[42] U.S. Senate, *Senate Report No. 427*, 46th Congress, 2nd Sess. (1880): 2–3.

[43] *Ibid.*, 2, 5.

[44] *Ibid.*, 11, 13.

[45] Ari Hoogenboom, *Outlawing the Spoils: A History of the Civil Service reform Movement, 1865–1883* (Westport: Greenwood Press, 1982), 225.

[party] workers, it may well be that they will have to be purchased in blocks of fives or blocks of tens."[46]

Another election-day abuse made more difficult by ballot reform was employer coercion of employees. The economic intimidation of factory workers in the North attracted less attention from reformers and Congress than did the violent "bulldozing" of black voters in the South. But the same short-lived Senate Democratic majority that investigated GOP political assessments also investigated employer intimidation in Massachusetts and Rhode Island in 1878. The committee looked into several reports of what witnesses and newspapers called "civilized bulldozing," which was said to be "much more frequent and effective in the manufacturing villages than in the cities."[47] Republicans assailed the committee for investigating activities in "these ancient and hitherto honored commonwealths" instead of Democratic abuses in the South. They characterized the 1878 Massachusetts gubernatorial election, which included a Greenback party candidate, as having pitted the forces of "social stability . . . prosperity and honor" against "repudiation, communism, and ruin." They denied that Republican party meetings to urge employers "to exert all the good influence possible upon employés" resulted in any intimidation. "There was some complaint that it 'dampened the ardor' of the employés, &c., but the weight of the evidence is overwhelming that it was simply the cooling-off process of returning reason which reduced the Democratic enthusiasm, and that upon sober second thought the intelligent workman realized the unity of his interests with those of the employer."[48]

This problem did not entirely escape the attention of reformers. Nine years after the committee's investigations, at least one reform-minded magazine remarked in an editorial that the ballot reform laws then sweeping the country would ensure that "the bulldozing employer cannot intimidate his employees to vote in accordance with his wishes."[49] *The New Englander and Yale Review* observed that Connecticut enacted its secret ballot law partly in response to 25 years worth of "complaints . . . made from time to time from some towns in the state that employers intimidated their employees, and required them to vote an open ballot under the inspection of someone representing the employer."[50]

---

[46]Jeremiah W. Jenks, "Money in Practical Politics," *The Century* (March 1894): 941.
[47]U.S. Senate, *Senate Report No. 497*, 46th Congress, 2nd Sess. (1880): 2–3.
[48]*Ibid.*, 12, 13, 15–16.
[49]"Ballot Reform Progress," *The Century* 38 (1889): 794
[50]*The New Englander and Yale Review*, vol., 52, No. 242 (May 1890): 402.

Why Were the Laws Passed?

Political Assessments

The assassination of President James A. Garfield in 1881 was the crucial event that broadened the appeal of the civil service reform movement. Garfield's assassin, although clearly unbalanced, was described as a disappointed office-seeker, one of the most familiar of 19th-century political types. The assassination energized reform organizations, which sent representatives to a national conference just one month after Garfield was shot. The conference vowed to work "in the press, on the platform, and by petition" to pass the Pendleton bill, and created the National Civil Service Reform League to facilitate united action. The following months saw the formation of new reform associations across the country.[51] Even the rapid growth of the reform movement was not enough to immediately move politicians whose careers and livelihoods had for years depended on the patronage system. They did enact reform, but they moved slowly and without Garfield's assassination they might not have moved at all.

Bribery and Intimidation of Voters

Impressed by the apparent success of the series of British corrupt practices acts that had been enacted from 1854 to 1883, reformers looked to Britain for guidance in writing reform legislation. Britain had adopted the Australian ballot law in 1872, and its 1883 act was praised as "a model for all countries having representative institutions."[52]

American adoption of the Australian law was triggered by the first presidential campaign finance scandal, in the 1888 election. The incumbent was Grover Cleveland, whose 1884 victory was the first the Democrats had won since 1856. For the first time since the birth of the GOP, the two parties were contesting the presidency on an equal footing. Both parties naturally spent heavily in swing states, and the "blocks of five" letter was only the most prominent of reports that vote buying had attained new highs in that election. James Bryce described the election as "one of the worst on record, so large was the expenditure in doubtful States. In that year well-informed Americans came to perceive that bribery at elections was a growing evil in their country. . . . This alarm has favoured the movement for the enactment of laws against corrupt practices."[53] Once states began enacting ballot reform laws, the movement swept the country. Massachusetts was the first state to enact an Australian ballot law, in 1888. Within three years, 32 more states had done so. By the end of the century all but six states had enacted ballot reform.

---

[51]Hoogenboom, *Outlawing the Spoils*, 209–13.
[52]E. L. Godkin, editorial, *The Nation*, Nov. 11, 1886, 387.
[53]James Bryce, *The American Commonwealth*, 3rd edition (New York: Macmillan, 1903), 2: 148.

The Knights of Labor were among the most active supporters of Australian Ballot laws, but bribery was not their chief concern. The Knights' Grand Master Workman Terence Powderly argued that the secret ballot would end employers' practice of sending superintendents and foremen to the polls to hand out Republican party ballots to their workers.[54]

Did the Laws Work as Intended?

Political Assessments

By the end of the 19th century, the Pendleton Act, which covered only 10 percent of federal employees on enactment, was expanded to cover more than 40 percent. Political assessments of government employees at various levels of government continued through the New Deal, but by then were much less important as a source of party campaign funds, at least at the federal level. Reform laws can take only part of the credit for this success. The growing industrial economy, and the government's growing role in it, made a professional civil service an economic as well as political necessity. Political appointment of every office down to small-town postmasters, and the creation of a class of indentured political servants to fill those offices, was not compatible with the demands on a government that was being called upon to adopt "business" methods.

Economic trends cannot take credit for the Pendleton Act—it was forced on Congress by a political crisis. But, as Nelson W. Polsby tells us of our own time, "A crisis can get a policy enacted but it cannot make the policy actually work afterward."[55] Political parties renounced assessments only when they could replace them. Little more than a decade after passage of the Pendleton Act, contributions from corporations and from the wealthy owners, investors, and managers of those corporations had become the major source of party campaign funds. Reform succeeded because it complemented larger social and economic changes.

Bribery and Intimidation of Voters

It's likely that Australian ballot laws did more to reduce "bulldozing" by employers than the bribery of voters. The reason for the difference between the two is that much of what we now consider bribery really was something else. The people who had no partisan loyalties and auctioned their vote to the highest bidder always were a tiny minority of voters. More common were voters who were loyal supporters of a party but who expected some payment, as compensation for making the trip into town on election day or simply as recognition for

---

[54]*New York Times,* January 2, 1890, 1.

[55]Nelson W. Polsby, *Political Innovation* (New Haven: Yale University Press, 1984), 169.

their loyalty. In this sense, party payments to voters, and treating them in saloons, reflected a vestige of 18th-century paternalism.

Party loyalties in the Gilded Age were less the result of voters' policy convictions than groupings of ethnic, religious, occupational, and other loyalties. The decreasing importance of bribery at the polls probably had far more to do with the waning of this kind of tribalism than with antibribery laws or ballot reform.[56] As with political assessments, the demise of this campaign finance practice was not legislated but came about as the result of larger political changes.

What Ideas of Good Government Motivated Supporters and Opponents?

Reformers rarely debated philosophies of government with their opponents. Unlike 18th-century Virginia, where there was no debate because the planter gentry's idea of good government was unchallenged, debate was absent in the Gilded Age because only one side was inclined to argue. Reformers had no shortage of principled arguments against assessments and the bribery and intimidation of voters, but their opponents were not eager to defend these practices. Instead of a debate, there were insistent demands for change from reformers and mostly silent resistance in Congress and the state legislatures.

Reformers were energetic in this one-sided debate because they put themselves squarely at the center of their own idea of good government. "[W]hat they meant by 'honest, efficient public service' was government by an elite class of men like themselves."[57] The chief obstacles to the reformers' ideal state were the political bosses who had usurped what the reformers saw as their rightful place in American government and politics. The two campaign finance measures discussed here were aimed at what reformers saw as the main supports of machine politics: the spoils system and the "ignorant and grossly corrupt persons" who made up "a very large proportion of our voters."[58]

Many, perhaps most, reformers opposed universal manhood suffrage, which they believed had caused democracy to careen out of control. Historian Francis Parkman, for example, warned that society was no longer in danger from tyrants or kings: "the real tyrant is organized ignorance, led by unscrupulous craft, and marching, amid the applause of fools, under the flag of equal rights."[59] Reform-

---

[56]Michael Schudson, *The Good Citizen: A History of American Civic Life* (Cambridge, Mass.: Harvard University Press, 1998), 144–74.

[57]John G. Sproat, *"The Best Men"* (London: Oxford University Press, 1968), 270.

[58]E. L. Godkin, editorial, *The Nation,* Jan. 24, 1875, 406.

[59]Francis Parkman, "The Failure of Universal Suffrage," *The North American Review* 127 (1878): 2.

ers even attempted to re-impose property or education requirements, which would have been a kind of campaign finance reform in reverse. They soon realized that their vision of a restricted electorate was not widely shared and that rolling back universal manhood suffrage was politically impossible.

Civil service reform had broader support, not least within the civil service itself. Although the success of this reform would leave universal suffrage intact, it promised to deprive parties of much of their money. This is what would have happened had reform not coincided with the ability of parties to raise even more money from business. Businessmen were a huge disappointment for reformers. Godkin was already voicing his dismay shortly after the end of the Civil War, lamenting the "connection of commercial immorality, that is, of haste and unscrupulousness in money-getting, with political corruption."[60] Twenty years later, Carl Schurz, a leading Mugwump and one of the founders of the Republican party, described the link between business and politics: "Great industrial interests are built up, fostered, and benefited by national legislation. . . . They are called upon by the managers of a political party to contribute large sums of money. . . . A considerable part of the money contributed by them is used in purchasing votes for the purpose of carrying the election and then controlling the Government for their benefit."[61] In this respect, at least, there is a surface appearance of agreement between reformers and the labor organizations that campaigned for the Australian ballot. As Powderly explained the cause to a labor meeting in 1890, without the secret ballot, "the moneyed men would control all and own all."[62]

But while reformers may have been disappointed with businessmen, even contemptuous of the newly rich tycoons, they feared and despised the "dangerous classes." Godkin regularly attacked the Knights in his *Nation* editorials, and called "The great corporations . . . the greatest benefactors the laborer has had in this country."[63] The reformers' status resentments and backward-looking political theories have been covered extensively in the historical literature and need no further discussion here. Suffice it to say that the success of the reforms they promoted did nothing to broaden the appeal of their idea of good government. Organized labor fared no better, as the fear that "moneyed men would control all" did not vanish with the success of reform.

---

[60]E. L. Godkin, "Commercial Immorality and Political Corruption" *The North American Review* 107 (1868): 255.

[61]*New York Times,* January 13, 1889, 16.

[62]*New York Times,* March 11, 1890, 5.

[63]E. L. Godkin, editorial, *The Nation,* Nov. 11, 1886, 386–87.

Conclusion

How well do the historical arguments about political money and reform stand up in the context of these glimpses into two widely separated periods of campaign finance history? One of those arguments rests on the claim that big money in politics is a relatively recent development that has increased political corruption. In this view, laws to curb the power of wealth are necessary to counter this threat to our democracy. The opposing argument rests on the claim that there always has been big money in politics but that it is a less corrupting force now than in the past. In this view, laws to curb the power of wealth are at best futile and at worst are themselves threats to democracy.

Has There Always Been Big Money in Elections or Is It a Recent Development?

There always has been money in elections, but it hasn't always played the same role. George Washington and other 18th-century candidates clearly spent large sums of money to get elected. But it was their money. At the time, it was impossible to separate election money from election candidates. The separation between money and candidates began in the early 19th century, especially in the North. There were many sources of political money then, including the personal funds of candidates from traditional social elites, contributions from wealthy individuals, "fees" from business interests seeking legislation, and government contracts to party newspapers. Only in the late 19th century, with the rise of large corporations as the primary source of party money, did the separation between candidates and the source of their money become an important feature of our politics. Money then came to be seen as a political force in its own right, but one originating "outside" politics. It is this development that explains why "money in politics" came to be a public policy concern.

If There Has Always Been Money in Politics, Have Attempts to Regulate Political Money Always Been Futile?

Just as the political role played by money has changed, so too has the political aim of campaign finance law. A relatively small, close-knit ruling class used the 18th-century Virginia laws to set the rules for its own behavior. Gentry politicians were protecting their collective self-interest by prohibiting the desperate or unethical actions of their individual members. The decision not to prohibit or even regulate other actions was another way the planter gentry protected its collective interest. They did not restrict the amount of money they could spend on their own campaigns. The 1752 attempt to impose restrictions on treating did not win enough support to become law. Nor were there any laws prohibiting Washington—who in 1758 was a colonel on active duty in the French and Indian War—from using his military subordinates as campaign workers. For example, the man who bought liquor for the election day treating was a lieutenant under Washington's command and was privately employed by him to supervise one of his plantations. Commenting on this arrangement, Flexner noted, "The distinction, so sharp in modern ethics, between a man's personal and his business affairs was dim according to the aristocratic mores Washington followed."[64]

The 18th-century Virginia campaign finance laws worked because they prohibited actions that occurred, almost by definition, at the margins of election campaigns. But as politicians came to be separated from the sources of their campaign money, once-deferential citizens came to look askance at both. As public opinion became a force in its own right, the regulation of campaign funding came to be seen less as a form of preventive maintenance of an existing system and more as "reform," i.e., as a way of changing that system to make it more open and democratic. For example, as government employees became an even more important political resource, public scrutiny of the way parties used them increased. Party organization may have replaced personal wealth and social status as the determinant of electoral success, but the patronage system seems to have updated rather than supplanted the old aristocratic idea that government was the collective property of the governors. During the 1867 debate over prohibiting the solicitation of campaign contributions from navy yard workers, Senator Timothy O. Howe (R-Wisc.) said those employees were "the creatures of the head of the Department; and if he wants them to do one kind of work, they shall do it . . . if he wants them to black boots, they shall black boots; if he wants them to pay money, they shall pay money."[65] Political assessments can be seen as an adaptation of anachronistic patron-client relationships to the era of organized parties and professional politicians. As they grew in importance in the campaign finance system, so too did popular doubts as to their propriety.

These doubts caused Gilded Age politicians who relied on assessments to at least make a show of restricting their own access to them. And as long as they continued to rely on assessments, a show was all they would make. Which is why civil service reform was futile until the appearance of another, more bountiful, source of funds coincided with a political crisis that could be addressed by enacting reform. Reform also was the answer to the political crisis arising out of the 1888 election, the first presidential campaign funding scandal. Neither bribery nor intimidation of voters was central to American or British politics at any period. But neither were they something that a politician would willingly forgo

---

[64] James Thomas Flexner, *George Washington: The Forge of Experience, 1732–1775* (Boston: Little, Brown, 1965), 280n.

[65] *Congressional Globe*, 39th Cong., 2nd Sess., March 1, 1967, p. 1948.

in a close election, which is why laws against it were futile until the enactment of Australian ballot laws became a political necessity for politicians who wanted to be on the right side of public disgust with corrupt practices. Another reason these laws worked is that they did not regulate the behavior of private citizens. Reformers were able to eliminate assessments as a source of campaign funds because the Pendleton Act changed the way government operated. The secret ballot worked because, in both its early and late 19th-century forms, it changed the way governments administered elections.

If Attempts to Regulate Political Money Were Not Always Futile, Did They Strengthen or Endanger Democracy?

Virginia's gentry politicians could be sure they were strengthening democracy with their laws because they were the authoritative source on what democracy meant at the time. Reformers in the Gilded Age were similarly certain that the laws they advocated would strengthen democracy, even though the United States had by then become far too complex and democratic to accept a single authority on how it define itself. Looking back, most people today would agree with both judgments. It's not clear, though, that George Washington and his contemporaries would have approved of the Gilded Age reforms, or that the Gilded Age reformers would have approved of ours. The Australian ballot, for example, would have been seen as a threat to the deferential democracies of the 18th century. Montesquieu called public voting "a fundamental law of democracy. The lesser people must be enlightened by the principal people and subdued by the gravity of certain eminent men." More than a century later, John Stuart Mill used an updated version of this argument to oppose the secret ballot, even as an antibribery measure: "The operation of the Ballot is, that it enables the voter to give full effect to his own private preferences . . . under no inducement to defer to the opinions or wishes of others. . . . Thirty years ago it was still true that . . . the main evil to be guarded against was that which the ballot would exclude—coercion by landlords, employers, and customers. At present, I conceive, a much greater source of evil is the selfishness . . . of the voter himself."[66]

The reason for these differences lies in changing ideas about the proper role of wealth in a democracy. As a public policy issue, campaign finance always has been more about control than accounting. Behind the question of how money should be used in elections there always has been the question of whose money should be used. This was true even in colonial Virginia, where the planter gentry had little trouble answering both questions. Not that the latter question was ever raised. That the gentry—the "best men" of their day—would provide the money

---

[66]John Stuart Mill, *Thoughts on Parliamentary Reform,* 2nd edition (London: John W. Parker and Son, 1859), 29, 31.

and the candidates was never in doubt. The Gilded Age reformers wanted to restore the rule of "the best men." A large part of their purpose in promoting civil service and ballot reform was to eliminate political machines as obstacles to that restoration. But most Americans did not share the reformers' backward-looking idea of democracy, which is why they failed to attain their political goals even as they achieved legislative success.

The colonial Virginia gentry acted to preserve the legitimacy of their rule. Although political legitimacy was a more complicated matter in the 1880s, the reforms of those years can be seen in the same way. Most Americans remained loyal to one or another of the major parties, but they no longer saw the patronage and party ballot systems as legitimate foundations for the governments those parties would form. Reforming those systems helped preserve the legitimacy of party rule. What the Gilded Age reforms did not do was settle the question of whose money should finance party democracy. Even general agreement on where this money should not come from—the pockets of government employees —did not begin to affect the financing of election campaigns until a new source of funds became available. The growing importance of corporations as a source of political funds soon gave rise to the concerns that continue to fuel the campaign finance debate today.

The origins of today's debate can be traced to 1897 state laws prohibiting corporations from making campaign contributions. In 1907, Congress passed a ban on such contributions as the first federal campaign finance law.[67] As the first laws to place restrictions on private sources of political funds and the first to target what had become the core of the campaign finance system, these laws marked a significant departure from the previous 200 years. The name of that 1907 law, however, suggested that Congress saw continuity with earlier legislation. It was called a "corrupt practices act," as was the 1925 law that revised and recodified the federal laws enacted in the previous 18 years. Corporate political contributions, however, have nothing in common with such corrupt practices as fraud, bribery, and intimidation at the polls. Rather, the objection to them is that they do not square with a particular idea of democracy. This kind of objection has defined the campaign finance debate for more than a century.

The goal of furthering some idea of democracy lay behind all the campaign finance laws discussed here. The difference between the laws enacted up to 1897 and those enacted since is that debates over the earlier laws took place within one generally accepted idea. It's true that the post-Civil War decades saw much more debate over the nature of democracy than existed in colonial Virginia. But the debates over civil service and ballot reform were not part of that larger philosophical argument. These reforms were accepted because they fell within the area of overlap among competing notions of democracy.

---

[67]Mutch, *Campaigns, Congress, and Courts*, xvii, 1–8.

Today's campaign finance debate is about restrictions on sources and amounts of political money, measures that do not fit neatly into that overlapping area. This debate has become so tangled because it's about theories of democracy, but is being conducted in terms of constitutional law. That's not an efficient way to debate political philosophy because constitutions are themselves the products of political philosophy. But it's because the debate reaches so deeply into the foundations of our system that we find it politically necessary to conduct it according to well-established legal procedures for handling issues that do not call fundamentals into question.

"Corruption" is the concern raised today, as it has been throughout the years discussed above. To George Washington and his contemporaries, corruption in campaign finance meant fraud, bribery, and intimidation at the polls. In the Gilded Age the word referred to these practices as well as to bribery of candidates and officeholders. All these practices have long been illegal and fall squarely within the jurisdiction of the courts. Which may be why even the Supreme Court continues to use the prevention of corruption as the rationale for its decisions in campaign finance cases even when that term is being used as an epithet for the political power of money. There is precedent for this: Insisting that a debate about democratic theory really is about corruption is like calling a ban on corporate political contributions a corrupt practices act.

But ideas of democracy change. The difference between the 18th-century Virginia campaign finance laws and those of our own time is that theirs were intended to protect the rule of wealth and ours are intended to prevent it. A century's worth of experience with these laws provides little reason to believe they will achieve their aim anytime soon. But we hold our democracy to higher standards than we did 300 or even 100 years ago, so concern about the political role of wealth will not be waning soon.

Chapter 2

Corruption and the Growth of Campaign Spending

Stephen Ansolabehere
Alan Gerber
James M. Snyder, Jr.

An important rationale for campaign finance reform in the United States today is the apparent failure of the existing system of contribution limits and public disclosure to stem corruption, or the appearance of corruption. The grant of political favors to campaign donors is widely seen as an increasingly serious problem for our society. Through their campaign donations, special interests have reputedly captured government, thereby gaining large economic favors in various forms, such as government contracts, tax breaks, and property right protection. As campaign spending has grown—and it has grown at an alarming rate—corruption has grown apace, according to reformers.

The argument can be summarized in a simple syllogism.
1. Campaign donations buy favors for special interests that give money to politics.
2. Campaign spending has risen dramatically over the last quarter century.
3. Therefore, corruption has risen dramatically.

We call this the Common Cause syllogism, since that interest group has pounded away at this critique for the better part of the last two decades, with a steady flow of studies and press releases rooting out shady practices and documenting the continued rise of special interest money in politics.[1] Dogged as Common Cause has been, they are not alone. Indeed, theirs is the view most widely held by public interest groups involved in campaign finance, such as the Center for Responsive Politics and Public Campaign. A sampling of books by Thomas Edsall, Brooks Jackson, Elizabeth Drew, and other reporters who cover the topic, reveals that most journalists also embrace this view.[2] And, more and more, the rhetoric has found its way into election campaigns themselves, with "outsiders" such as Bill Bradley and John McCain making campaign finance reform a central theme of their presidential candidacies.

The wide acceptance of the argument underscores its importance in the public discussion of campaign finance. Our aim is not to debate the premises behind the Common Cause syllogism.

Indeed, it seems right. Campaign spending has risen at an alarming rate over the two and a half decades since FECA was implemented. And, in a private system of campaign finance some degree of exchange of political support for donors is inevitable. Even the Court recognized the potential for corruption in a private system, noting in *Buckley v. Valeo* instances of favor selling from the 1972 presidential election. Continued growth in campaign spending in the years since *Buckley* is taken as evidence that corrupt practices are a growing problem in the United States. Throughout the 1980s, incumbent legislators raised increasingly large amounts of money from interested donors, especially through political action committees. In the 1990s, this "cancer" has spread from candidates to the parties in the form of soft money.[3]

So, rather than question the premises behind the Common Cause syllogism, our goal is to assess the importance of this argument. If donors indeed command favors in return for their contributions, then rising real campaign expenditures mean that corruption is growing out of control. Rising corruption leads to less efficiency in the economy, eventually producing lower growth. Social scientists, for their part, have had very little to say about corruption. Numerous studies have attempted, largely without success, to find the smoking gun behind specific pieces of legislation. However, few scholars have attempted to take a broader view of the matter. How should we judge the alarming escalation in campaign

---

[1] For example, see the reports on Common Cause's web site: www.commoncause. org.

[2] It is also the case that the amount of press devoted to the issue has risen 10 fold, from approximately 20 to 25 stories per year in the early 1980s in the *New York Times, Washington Post,* and *L.A. Times,* to 250 to 300 stories per year in the late 1990s.

[3] Sorauf (1992) provides an excellent survey of the scholarly and popular literature related to this matter.

spending? How accurate is the perception that corruption has become a bigger problem?

At stake are three fundamental issues. First, do we need a new campaign system? Twenty-five years ago, the United States implemented a private system of campaign financing which, through contribution limits and full public disclosure, was designed to constrain, even eliminate corrupt practices. Skyrocketing expenditures are taken as the first and most alarming piece of evidence that this system has failed to contain corrupt practices. But, what are the social costs associated with our system of private campaign finance? If those costs are substantial and are not contained by the existing system of limits and public disclosure, then some new sort of scheme is needed.

Second, do we need a new legal framework? In *Buckley v. Valeo*, the Supreme Court laid out a tradeoff between the speech rights of individuals and the governmental interest in limiting corruption or the appearance of corruption. The Court struck down spending limits as a violation of speech rights, but upheld the contribution limits of FECA as essential to limiting corruption. This ruling serves as the framework within which the Court views campaign finance in the U.S. today. Trends in real campaign spending are widely taken as evidence that the majority's decision in *Buckley* is simply out of date. Growing real campaign spending, and with it the increased social costs of corruption, have upset the balance that the Court originally saw in the system. The system of private fundraising within contribution limits has reputedly failed. And its failure, if real, calls into doubt the basic reasoning employed by the Court in *Buckley*. A new standard may be needed in order to deal adequately with questions of corruption. Such is the reasoning behind the concurring opinion in *Nixon v. Shrink Missouri*, which proposed political equality as an additional principle justifying regulation of campaign finance.

Third, have Americans conceived of interest group politics correctly? The majority in *Buckley* tacitly embraced a pluralist or Madisonian vision of politics: free and open competition among interests, a critical media, and electoral competition prevent any one interest from gaining substantial influence over public policy. But, critics argue, this view is founded on a belief in plural politics that don't work or are increasingly eclipsed by clientelism. Campaign finance reform may therefore be the opening to even more sweeping political reforms, including the introduction of proportional representation and lowering the barriers to third parties.

Such is the thinking of many critics of campaign finance today. We argue that this view is incorrect. Corruption, at least that produced through the campaign finance system, has not become a bigger problem for American society over the decades since *Buckley*. The reason is simple. The right baseline against which to measure the cost of corruption to society is the national income. And relative to the national income campaign spending has not grown.

Our argument is heretical, especially for three Democrats, and it deserves careful development. We proceed in three steps. First, we examine the trends in spending and their relationship to the economy. Second, we consider what is the right baseline against which to measure the growth in spending. Third, we present a simple model to analyze the logical relationship between rising spending and rising corruption.

Using the simple analytical framework presented, we consider the claim that the value of favors bought by campaign contributions is very large. This claim, we conclude, doesn't add up economically. We estimate that campaign contributions buy no more than $3 billion worth of economic favors for special interests, and that figure arises only if campaign contributions are an exceedingly profitable investment. In the abstract the $3 billion figure may sound large, but as a social problem it is small—less that three hundredths of a percent of the national income.

Has Spending Really Grown?

Our contention is that campaign spending has not really grown: it has expanded at the same rate as the national income. The perception that campaign spending is on the rise comes from reports of nominal campaign expenditures. Over time, the amounts spent on political campaigns have grown sharply: roughly 10 fold over the last 20 years. In 1978 the typical House incumbent spent approximately $75,000. By 1998, the typical incumbent spent approximately $650,000.

The following figures present two perspectives on campaign spending growth. The first plot shows the growth in campaign spending relative to the Consumer Price Index in the United States since the 1970s. There are three series: total spending in presidential election years, total spending in congressional elections, and total (hard and soft) party receipts. The data for total spending in presidential campaigns come from various publications of Herbert Alexander and his collaborators; they represent the best available estimates of total spending over this time span. The other figures come from the Federal Election Commissions' Reports on Financial Activity.

The trends are alarming. Campaign donations to every part of our government look to be growing without bound. Party money, congressional money, presidential money, and PAC contributions have all doubled over the last 25 years. Even our best efforts at public funding—the presidential campaign fund—have evidently been overrun by the private system. Now consider a second plot. Instead of dividing by CPI, normalize campaign spending using Gross Domestic Product, a measure of the value of all goods and services sold in the

Figure 2.1. Spending Over Time in Real 1998 Dollars

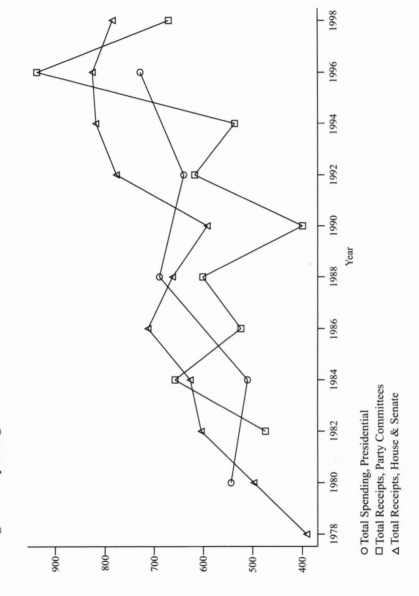

Millions of 1998 Dollars

Year

○ Total Spending, Presidential
□ Total Receipts, Party Committees
△ Total Receipts, House & Senate

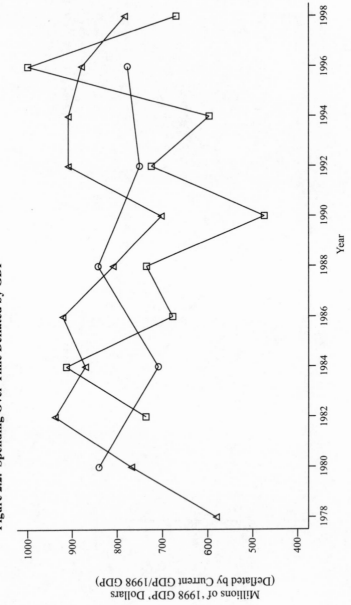

Figure 2.2. Spending Over Time Deflated by GDP

O Total Spending, Presidential
□ Total Receipts, Party Committees
△ Total Receipts, House & Senate

United States economy. Has the amount spent on campaigns—on democracy—risen faster than the amount spent on all manner of goods?

The trend vanishes. There are ups and downs associated with particular election years, but it is quite clear that campaign spending has not grown faster than the nation's income. Total campaign spending in presidential years hovers around one-hundredth of one percent of Gross Domestic Product. The presidential campaign fund has shrunk compared to the wealth of the economy because the Federal Elections Campaign Act pegged those funds to the Consumer Price Index. Even political party receipts, the target of the most recent reform efforts, have shown no growth compared to GDP.

One caveat to these data is in order. The figures may underreport some campaign activities, such as issue advocacy by groups. Such figures are unknown, though attempts to estimate these activities have been made using media advertising data. Estimates hover in the range of $100 million in 1996. Adding these numbers to the total campaign spending in 1996 changes the pattern little: total campaign spending has risen at the same rate as the GDP.

Political Action Committee (PAC) money—a measure of special interest money—has also shown little growth relative to the economy. Table 2.1 presents average and total PAC contributions to congressional candidates from 1978 to 1998. The second and third columns of the table present the average corporate PAC contribution to all U.S. House candidates from 1978 to 1996.

We have selected corporations because they are widely considered to be the "investors" in politics; similar patterns hold for unions, trade and membership associations, and nonconnected PACs. We have isolated the House because the Senate data vary somewhat depending on which states are up. The average nominal corporate contribution has skyrocketed, growing from about $400 in 1978 and 1980 to $1,200 in 1994 and 1996, combined. Relative to GDP, however, the average contribution is unchanged, hovering around $460 dollars in terms of 1980 GDP.

Since the early 1980s, total PAC receipts have not grown faster than the GDP. They have even shrunk somewhat since the mid-1980s. The fourth and fifth columns of Table 2.1 present total PAC contributions to congressional candidates deflated by CPI and by GDP, respectively. The fourth column presents PAC contributions in real 1998 dollars. The fifth column presents total contributions deflated by current GDP relative to 1998 GDP. Total PAC contributions were lower in 1978 and 1980 than in subsequent years. The late 1970s apparently witnessed sharp growth in PACs as the legality of them as a mode of giving was in doubt until late 1976. But since 1980, the figure has hovered around $200 million in 1998 GDP deflated dollars.

The pattern seems to travel well, too. California and the United Kingdom provide excellent contrasts. Boasting a very active and professional state government, California has an unregulated campaign finance system, but it has provided for full public disclosure of campaign contributions and expenditures

Table 2.1. PAC Contributions to Congressional Candidates, 1978 to 1996

Year	Avg. Contrib. Current Dollars	GDP Deflated (1980 + 1)	Total Contribs. 1998 CPI Defl. (millions)	Total Contribs. 1998 GDP Defl. (millions)
1978	$356.50	$433.17	$ 79.26	$117.76
1980	440.09	440.09	109.23	168.79
1982	537.99	462.01	1.24	219.52
1984	609.73	435.02	165.24	229.72
1986	697.60	439.21	197.31	255.34
1988	810.61	446.95	203.37	249.19
1990	952.36	461.64	182.94	217.35
1992	1105.77	493.03	203.37	238.59
1994	1139.48	456.68	293.53	215.57
1996	1284.12	466.64	204.95	219.15
1998			203.02	203.0123

since the mid-1970s.[4] The state imposes no limits on contributions and offers no public money to candidates: it's the Wild West.[5] A number of publications by a public watchdog organization, the California Committee on Campaign Finance, document that campaign spending in California has risen much faster than the Consumer Price Index. In it's report *The New California Gold Rush,* the California Committee on Campaign Finance summarizes the "Skyrocketing Campaign Costs" as follows: "In 1958 all legislative races in California cost a total of $1.4 million. In 1984 these same races cost $44.8 (an increase of 3,100% in

---

[4]Disclosure was overseen by an agency, the Fair Political Practices Commission, from the 1970s through 1990. In 1990, disclosure shifted from the Fair Political Practices Commission to the Secretary of State's office. The FPPC now handles ethics investigations only. The Secretary of State has done a good job at disclosure. They offer summary reports of expenditures and receipts, with comparisons over time, and electronic disclosure in 2000.

[5]California has attempted regulation of political contributions several times, including in 1990 and 1997, but the courts have struck down the limits passed by the public.

26 years) . . . California's rising campaign costs have outstripped inflation and population growth."[6]

Spending has not, however, grown faster than the state's income. Figure 3 graphs expenditures on state legislative and on gubernatorial races, divided by the state's domestic product.

The United Kingdom limits candidate spending, and has since 1883, but it imposes no limits on party spending or fundraising practices. Indeed, that system was in many ways the blueprint for the Federal Elections Campaign Act.[7] Low limits on candidates' campaign expenditures imposed by Parliament in 1883, however, have shifted the burden of campaign fundraising and spending from individual politicians to the party organizations. Since the mid-1960s, the combined candidate and party expenditures have grown more than treble the CPI in the U.K. However, as with spending at the U.S. national level and in California, party and candidate spending in the U.K. have just kept pace with the growth in income.[8]

Finally, historical data on campaign spending in national elections provide tantalizing evidence of the robustness of this regularity. Louise Overacker provides one of the first systematic studies of money in American elections. Relying on reports to the clerk of the House, she documents that from 1912 to 1928, two decades of remarkable economic growth, spending by parties on national elections accounted for .008 percent of national income and remained steady over the five presidential elections examined (Overacker 1934, 78). Oddly, the point seems to have been largely dropped by subsequent scholarly and popular writers. The pattern she observed, though, seems just as apt today. Campaign spending tends to go up at the same pace as the national income, which rises faster than the Consumer Price Index.[9]

---

[6]California Commission on Campaign Finance, *The New Gold Rush: Financing California's Legislative Campaigns* (Los Angeles, Calif.: Center for Responsive Government, 1985).

[7]The British law is even the *locus classicus* of the legal entity of a separate and segregated fund through which organized interests such as unions and corporations may give to candidates: in common parlance, a PAC.

[8]Figures come from Richard Katz and Peter Mair, eds., *Party Organizations: A Data Handbook* (London: Sage, 1992), and David M. Farrell and Paul Webb, "Political Parties as Campaign Organizations," in *Parties Without Partisans,* ed. Russell Dalton and Martin P. Wattenberg (New York: Oxford University Press, 1999).

[9]In relation to the GDP of the time, this figure is actually somewhat larger than today's campaign expenditures. Total campaign spending amounts to $1.5 billion out of an $8 trillion economy.

Figure 2.3. Trends in Total Campaign Expenditures in California Elections

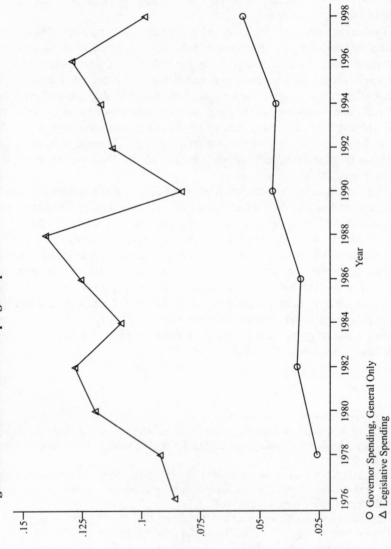

O Governor Spending, General Only
△ Legislative Spending

Two Questions, Two Metrics

Price growth and income growth offer two very different standards against which to gauge trends in campaign spending. Which metric is the right one? Both are, but they are revealing about different questions. A continual point of confusion in the interpretation of trends in campaign spending data is the baseline against which changes in expenditures should be measured. Some deflation seems necessary—the dollar today is simply not what it was in 1975 or 1950. Most scholars deflate by the Consumer Price Index. Some, especially in the comparative literature, divide by population or votes cast. A few have discussed the pattern after dividing by national income, though little is made about the flatness of the graphs when spending is divided by income. Ambiguity about the appropriate baseline, though, has led some observers and researchers not to deflate data at all. The upward trends in spending, of course, are most dramatic in nominal or current dollars.

What baseline one uses depends, ultimately, on what question is at stake. If the effects of rising spending on electoral competition are at issue, then the Consumer Price Index offers an appropriate standardization. If the relationship between campaign finance and corruption is at issue, then Gross Domestic Product is the right baseline. The reasons for this distinction are simple. Concerns about the effects of rising campaign spending on elections pertain to what the campaign dollar buys today, compared to, say, 20 years ago. The prices of most campaign inputs—labor, television airtime, office supplies—rise with the CPI. Take labor, for example. The Employment Compensation Index (or ECI) measures the increase in the typical employees' wages and benefits. Hourly wages in the United States have fallen in real terms since the late 1970s, but compensated income has risen at the same rate as the CPI. The ECI in 1998 was 1.65 times larger than the ECI in 1982; the CPI in 1998 was 1.63 times larger than the CPI in 1982.[10] The prices of television advertising time, of column inches of newspaper advertising, of outdoor advertising space, and of most other media have risen over the last 25 years at the same rate as inflation. The one commonly used campaign input that has seen price growth in excess of the CPI is direct mail. If spending is going up faster than the Consumer Price Index, then campaigns are simply buying more than they used to. In a separate paper, we calculate that campaigns are actually buying more minutes of television airtime than they did 25 years ago (Ansolabehere, Gerber, and Snyder 1999).

Concerns about corruption, ultimately, rest on whether corruption is a drag on the economy, whether we are wasting a large or increasing share of our economy. From that perspective the size of the economy is the relevant baseline.

---

[10]U.S. Census Bureau, The Statistical Abstract of the United States, 1999, Table 704 (page 446) and Table 796 (page 495).

If corruption rises more slowly than national wealth, then we will eventually grow out of the problem. If, for example, corruption is increasing at one dollar a day, but the economy grows by two dollars a day, then corruption will eventually become trivial. The problem is that if corruption grows faster than the economy, then it will eventually consume the economy.

This argument receives its most cogent expression in the writings of economists about the rent-seeking society (Tullock 1967; McChesney 1997). The government has legislative power, through both fiscal authority and regulatory authority, over the economy. Elected officials are the agents of the private economy (the voters) to produce the public good most efficiently. This agency relationship, though, is imperfect. Rent-seeking legislators will make inefficient laws that serve, in part, their private, reelection interests. The relevant concern then is this: what is the "agency" cost of governing the economy through this system of representation with private campaign finance? These costs are gauged in terms of the economy as a whole. We care, then, about what percentage of the economy is consumed by rent seeking; GDP is the appropriate gauge. CPI is an inappropriate baseline against which to measure corruption because the CPI captures price changes in an ideal bundle of consumer goods. It does not reflect changes in technology and the wealth that creates.

A Simple Model of Corruption, Growth, and Campaign Spending

What can we infer about corruption from the absence of growth in campaign spending relative to national income? On its face, the patterns we have presented suggest that the problems associated with corruption are not increasing; they are about the same as before. Taking the rhetoric of critics and reformers at face value, the pattern we observe suggests that corruption is no worse than it was 25 years ago, when FECA was in its infancy and when the Court ruled that the concerns about corruption did not outweigh individuals' speech rights.

Rhetorical twists and intuitions aside, under what conditions do increases in campaign spending reveal increasing corruption problems? Here we spell out the link between campaign spending growth and rising corruption explicitly. We begin with a few assumptions. First, following the critics of campaign finance, we assume that candidates raise money from interested donors by selling favors, such as tax breaks, government contracts, and regulatory relief. The dollar value of these favors is an unknown amount, but in economics the dollar value equals the price paid times the number of services sold or favors done. Second, assume that candidates receive a certain fraction of their favor sales in the form of campaign contributions. One might imagine, for example, that politicians and groups bargain over the amount of campaign money that will be exchanged for each favor. Groups would never pay more than the favor is worth, and candidates would never give away a favor for free. The candidate's return on a favor equals a share of the value of each favor, or if you like the price of a favor sold. Politicians keep a certain fraction of the value and donors get the rest. The total money raised by candidates for office, then, equals the candidates' "share" of each favor times the value of the favors.

In economic terms, such corruption is a growing problem if it is an increasing share of the economy. So, consider total favors sold as a fraction of the national income (or Gross Domestic Product). We then have the following identity relating the percent of national income spent on campaigns and the percent of national income lost to corruption. Total campaign contributions as a fraction of national income equals the "share" kept by candidates times the total value of favors sold as a fraction of national income.

We have observed that total campaign contributions are not increasing as a fraction of national income. What does that imply about the total value of favors sold?

The change in campaign spending relative to national income can be broken into two components: the change due to shifts in the "terms of trade" among politicians and donors and the change due to increases in the total value of favors sold relative to national income. It is the second term that is of economic or societal concern. If the second term is growing, then the society as a whole is losing income because of corruption. To put the matter another way, campaign contributions may grow because politicians receive more money for every favor they do or because there is more stuff to sell.

The terms of trade might change if either politicians or contributors gained more leverage relative to the other. For example, if politicians went from competing among themselves to acting like monopolists in granting favors, then politicians' could increase their share of the favors sold. This is the idea behind legislators increasingly "shaking down" donors for money. The value of favors sold relative to GDP might increase for a variety of reasons. For example, if government began to control a larger share of GDP, as might have occurred with the expansion of regulations in the 1970s, then the economic value of government activities to businesses and other "investors" might have grown.

If total campaign contributions have not grown relative to GDP, then two components must not change—the terms of trade and the value of services as a share of the total economy. A result in mathematics is that the total change in a product approximately equals the sum of the change in each component times the value of the other component. In our case, that means that the total change in campaign contributions is the sum of two components. The first component is the change in the share kept by politicians times the total value of favors sold. The second component is the change in the total value of favors sold times the share kept by politicians.

This argument carries several important lessons about the relationship between campaign contributions and corruption. Here, we consider two special cases. First, suppose that there is no change in campaign spending relative to national income. This is the situation documented above for the U.S., the U.K., and California.

In this case, corruption can grow faster than the economy only if the "terms of trade" become worse for the politicians, that is, if the donors somehow gain greater bargaining power. Suppose there has been no real growth in campaign spending. In order for the relationship sketched above to hold, any increase in the value of favors sold must be offset by a loss in the share kept by candidates. In other words, in this situation there is a negative association between the change in corruption and the change in the legislators' return on favors.

The last formulation means that a one percent increase in the value of services provided must correspond with a one percent *decrease* in the politicians return on favors sold. Obversely, if politicians get higher returns on their services, then corruption must fall. The change in the amount of corruption (the value of services sold by politicians) depends on changes in the politicians' bargaining power (and rates of return) *vis-à-vis* interest groups. These intuitions, again, emerge in the special case in which campaign spending grows at the same rate as national income.

A second important case arises when there is no change in the "terms of trade" between contributors and politicians. That is, suppose that over time candidates' keep the same share of revenues that they always do. Then, campaign spending will grow at the same rate as the value of favors being sold. In this situation, a significant increase in corruption (i.e., the amount of favors sold as a fraction of GDP) will increase campaign spending. Similarly, any significant change in campaign spending relative to national income indicates a real increase in corruption. This situation is tacitly assumed by observers who, upon noting growth in spending relative to the CPI, infer that corruption is an increasing problem.

The assumption that the "terms of trade" have not changed appreciably amounts to an important assumption behind most public discussions about campaign finance. It is hard to verify empirically with a simple graph, such as those mustered earlier. We believe, however, that this describes roughly the circumstances in American national politics over the last two decades. The terms of trade are influenced by the bargaining power of groups and politicians. If politicians gain more leverage in their dealings with potential donors, they can extract more "rents" for every dollar of favor sold. In the extreme, each politician acts like a monopolist *vis-à-vis* a large number of competing groups. Such is the case if politicians are able to "shake down" groups. If groups gain more leverage, then they can extract more dollars of favors for every dollar contributed. In the extreme, many politicians service each donor, and competition among the politicians for the donor's resources will bid down the return on each favor.

In reality, neither of the extreme conditions holds. Congress remains an institution in which power is widely held. Committee and subcommittee chairmen protect their terrain, and on many bills and oversight matters jurisdictions overlap and committees compete. Observers of D.C. politics over the last two dozen years describe an incredible pluralism, with considerable competition among groups and among politicians. In the early 1970s there was a rapid expansion in the number of groups participating in politics, driven in large part by the reaction of business groups against the implementation of new regulations. But, sometime around 1980, we seem to have reached a steady state in group competition.

There are approximately 2,000 active business PACs in Washington, D.C., and many more lobbying organizations. The typical House member receives contributions from about 200 PACs, and the typical contribution is approximately $1,200 today, as we saw in Table 1. Letting some of these donors "walk away from the table" would have negligible electoral consequences for a typical House incumbent. Both the average number of PAC donors and the average PAC contribution (relative to GDP) have not changed since 1980. It seems unlikely, then, that the leverage of any one contributor over a typical member of Congress has changed much over the last 20 years, and it may have even dropped since the 1970s when a somewhat smaller number of groups gave money to politics.

This, perhaps overly simplistic, view of national politics suggests that the terms of trade have not changed dramatically over the years considered in this study. If true, then the share of favors kept by politicians is likely a constant factor. Hence, recent trends in spending suggest that the fraction of the economy lost to favor selling has not risen since the late 1970s.

To the extent the balance of power between groups and politicians has changed, the shift may even be in the direction of the politicians. Much of the research and writing about interest group politics in the U.S. documents that the number of groups with representation in D.C. has grown substantially over the last 25 years. In other words, today there are more groups vying for the attention of politicians and for special treatment from the government than there were in the mid 1970s. More competition among groups increases the politicians' leverage and raises the price of a favor. Combined with the fact that campaign contributions have not grown faster than GDP, the observation that there are more groups in D.C. now than there were 25 years ago implies, paradoxically, that there is *less* corruption.

How Much Corruption?

One important remaining matter is the value of the favors sold through campaign contributions. If favor selling exacts a large economic cost, regardless of whether those costs are growing faster than the economy, then the public may still have an interest in containing corruption. Favor selling may produce large economic costs two ways. First, politicians may transfer very valuable goods to special interests. In other words, favors sold are private goods, and, through campaign donations, businesses and other investors buy special treatment that the market would never afford. Second, favor selling may generate large external costs. For example, a $2 million tax break for a private interest may mean that we spend $2 million less on a very valuable public good, in which the market tends to invest too little, but which produces substantial collective benefits to society.

The first of these arguments is that made by Common Cause and others and widely believed by the public and journalists: special interests benefit enormously from the campaign finance system. To put the matter bluntly, the criticism doesn't add up too much. Tullock (1972) calculated that the value of favors sold to rent-seeking contributors could account for no more than a tiny fraction of the overall economy. We offer a similar calculation here.

The simple model presented in the preceding section allows us to give a rough calculation of the potential economic value of favors sold to private interests through the campaign finance system. First, we can calculate the value of goods sold by reversing the equation above. Total campaign contributions equal the value of favors sold times the fraction kept by the candidates (the price). So, the total value of favors sold equals the total value of campaign contributions divided by the fraction kept by candidates (or the price). Second, we can calculate an approximate price by considering the investors' rate of return. The investors' rate of return is the price demanded by investors in order for them to be willing to invest in an asset. This rate of return relates to the fraction kept by donors directly. Specifically, the investors' return on their donations equals the ratio of the share kept by the investor to the share kept by the politician. If, for instance, the politician and the investor split the value of the favors sold equally, then the share kept by the politician is .5 and the rate of return is 100 percent (i.e., .5/.5). The investor, thus, gets two dollars for every dollar contributed to the politicians. If the politician keeps nothing, then the rate of return is infinite. If the politician keeps all, then the rate of return to the business is zero. Third, substituting a value for the rate of return, we can calculate a plausible upper bound for the total value of favors sold through the campaign finance system.

Federal campaign finance—including party and candidate funds— amounted to approximately $1.5 billion in 1996. To calculate the value of favors sold we divide total campaign contributions by the share kept by candidates.

Unfortunately, no social scientists have estimated the rate of return to campaign contributions. So we will use several possible values. It is plausible that the rate of return on campaign contributions is not too large, otherwise businesses and individuals would take their money out of the stock market and give it to politicians. Assuming a very lucrative rate of return of 100 percent to donors on each dollar contributed (that is, the share kept is .5), the implied total value of favors sold in 1996 was $3 billion. A more earthly rate of return of 20 percent (i.e., the politicians keep 5/6), which is in line with corporate rates of return, implies that the value of favors sold in 1996 was at most $1.8 billion.

Such calculations labor under the assumption that all of the money raised came from investors. Using just Political Action Committee donations and corporate donations to parties, total amount of "investor" campaign money at stake is just under $500 million. With a 100 percent rate of return on donors' investments, the value of favors sold is on the order of $1 billion. The nation's economy was valued at almost $8 trillion in 1996. Favor selling and corruption through the campaign finance system amounts to a trivial part of our economy—spare change in the national accounts.

The argument that the total value of favors sold is small assumes that political investment resembles other sorts of investment. A 100 percent rate of return on political contributions would look extremely lucrative in the world of private investment: it far exceeds that of stock markets and pretax corporate returns. Imperfections in the market might push the rate of return very high, as several formal theory papers argue. For example, Helpman and Grossman (1998) construct a model in which funds come from one donor and two legislators compete for the contribution. In such a world, the legislators bid down the price, until the policy is sold essentially for free. Such an argument rests on the assumption that there is no competition among groups for the specific policy or for the legislators' time.

This argument alone looks implausible. If the rate of return were exceptionally high, then businesses and wealthy individuals could shift their portfolios slightly in the direction of politics and earn rates far in excess of what they earn on their other investments. One commonly hears the question, among academics at least, "Why isn't there more money in politics?" The question expresses not a moral value, but a nagging doubt. If investment in politics were very lucrative then many more businesses and wealthy individuals would give, and they would each give much more. It is possible to sustain a model in which rates of return are very high, but one must make at least two more assumptions. First, there must be relatively low marginal costs of favor selling. For a large range of favors, the cost to the legislator of delivering the goods must be small; politicians must risk little political damage to selling billions of dollars in favors. Second, there must be relatively high inframarginal returns to donors. The first, say, $10,000 must bring a very high rate of return, but the ability to buy additional benefits drops very quickly after that.

The behavior of donors and legislators suggests that the returns to contributions are not exceptionally high. Businesses and individuals who do give rarely contribute the maximum allowed by law—$10,000 for groups and $2,000 for individuals in a primary and general election combined. The typical corporate gift is in the range of $1,200 in 1998 dollars. Further evidence that the rate of return on contributions is modest comes from what we know about congressional behavior generally. Many papers estimate the effects of contributions on parts of the process, especially roll call voting behavior. The effects are modest and uneven. Indeed, most analyses show no significant effects of interest group contributions on legislative outcomes. Legislative behavior tends to be motivated primarily by ideological, district oriented, and partisan, rather than campaign donations (Sorauf 1992).

Although the immediate value of favors sold appears small, our private system of campaign finance may still create substantial economic costs. Political decisions that benefit special interests may generate external costs, which are not realized by the donor or the politician. Politicians may get $1 billion in exchange for favors worth $2 to $3 billion to donors, but those favors might create economic inefficiencies that cost the society hundreds of billions, even trillions of dollars worth of growth. For example, the favors sold to one industry may mean that we invest less in activities that have extremely high social benefits.

The external economic costs of campaign contributions are an open matter. Given the small amount spent on campaigns, the only plausible way that the external social costs can be large is if the effects escalate or cause even more dramatic failures: "for want of a nail, the kingdom was lost."

Conclusion

Our basic point is that campaign spending is not growing out of control. It has grown steadily, at the same rate of growth as the economy as a whole. This fact turns the rhetoric of reformers on its head. Assuming the Common Cause syllogism is right, the corruption generated by campaign contributions is likely no worse of an economic problem today than it was 25 years ago, when FECA was in its infancy and when the Court ruled that the concerns about corruption did not outweigh individuals speech rights. There may be other strong reasons for wanting reform, such as political inequality or distortion of electoral competition. However, it is not evident that growing corruption provides a compelling rationale for campaign finance reform today.

Two features of the relationship between spending and GDP deserve closer attention: how broadly this pattern holds and why spending grows with GDP. Regarding the first question, cursory examination of several other OECD countries reveals the same pattern. There are problems with underreporting of campaign spending in the European countries, especially party money, so these analyses are difficult to make. The best European data come from the United Kingdom, and the pattern of spending in British parliamentary elections matches that in the U.S. What is most intriguing about the comparison between the U.K. and the U.S. is that the U.K. has a heavily regulated system, embracing many of the reforms sought in the U.S.—including spending limits on candidates and restrictions on television advertising. Nonetheless, spending grows apace with GDP in the U.K. Just like U.S. national elections. Regulation of the level of spending through limits and TV restrictions may, thus, be elusive.

The second matter—why spending grows with GDP—goes to the core of understanding money in American politics. The pattern may be explained two ways. We have embraced, for the sake of argument, the view that spending grows with the national income because the size of government, i.e., the amount of stuff available to be sold, and the income of those doing the buying also grow with GDP.[11] More income means more government activity, and more government activity means more favors to be done for special interests. Another account comes from studies of political participation. Campaign contributing is one form of voluntary participation in politics. As personal income rises, giving rises (Verba, Schlozman, and Brady 1995). The second explanation further weakens the corruption rationale for regulating political spending.

As a practical matter it is hard to untangle these effects. We have analyzed spending in gubernatorial elections using per capita income, per capita government spending, and population to explain total expenditures. It is nearly impossible to untangle the income and government spending effects because they are correlated within the states. We have further analyzed Senate expenditures and find that candidates for office in richer and bigger states spend much more and raise more from individuals, but they do not raise more from PACs than their counterparts in smaller states (Ansolabehere and Snyder 1999). This pattern suggests that both mechanisms—voluntary giving and *quid pro quo* giving—are at work. Which one acts, as a more important driver of the campaign finance system, remains to be resolved.

Our analysis also reveals the hidden logic behind arguments that corruption is a growing problem. In a world in which campaign spending has not grown faster than GDP, for the value of favors sold to have increased substantially faster than our wealth, the power of groups *vis-à-vis* politicians must have increased greatly as well. In other words, to be logically consistent, those who contend that corruption is an increasing problem must also document that politicians are taking a smaller "cut" (i.e., the share kept by politicians has dropped). For groups to be more powerful relative to politicians there must be less supply

---

[11]John R. Lott makes this argument ("A Simple Explanation for Why Campaign Expenditures are Increasing: The Government is Getting Bigger," unpublished manuscript).

of interest group money—i.e., fewer groups involved in campaign contribut-ing—or more demand for money by politicians—i.e., more electoral competi-tion.

We do not have direct evidence about this matter, because there are no so-cial science estimates of the politicians' and groups' rates of return on favors sold. But we do think that many critics err in their analyses of the present situa-tion. The argument of many critics is not only that the dollars have grown but that (1) the number of interests coming to D.C. seeking special treatment has expanded and (2) the "exchange" is increasingly led by incumbents, by a more limited set of sellers who are more secure and may thus have lower demand for money. Both arguments work against the notion that the interest groups get a larger fraction of the rents. As more groups compete for legislators' time, the price that legislators demand for a favor goes *up*. If there is significantly more group activity today, then the rate of return to groups has likely fallen. As Robert Salisbury observed, interest groups in D.C. are "awash in access but of-ten subordinate in influence." In a similar vein, it is observed that incumbents have increased political leverage in their dealings with groups. As incumbents become electorally safer and politically more powerful in Washington they have less need for aid from interested donors. The "rising power of incumbency," Frank Sorauf concluded, has meant the "shrinking power of PACs." (Sorauf 1992, 66). If incumbents are indeed in the cat-bird seat, then their leverage *vis-à-vis* groups has also risen. So, again, legislators can command larger donations for each favor granted.

Paradoxically, then, expansion of the number of groups in Washington poli-tics may work against their increased power. More groups bidding for favors and more secure incumbents mean that legislators today can command a larger fraction of the "rents" than they did 20 years ago. The fact that we observe no change in campaign donations relative to GDP means that the total value of fa-vors sold relative to the national income may have actually *dropped*. Corruption, at least the corruption that comes from campaign contributions, then is not a growing social or economic problem, and it may have even lessened over the last two decades.

Our analytical model further suggests that the value of favors sold through campaign contributions is likely very small relative to GDP. Assuming an ex-traordinary 100 percent rate of return and assuming that all contributions get some favor in return, the value of favors sold amounts to $3 billion, a negligible fraction of the U.S. economy.

Still, the perception that corruption is widespread and growing rapidly is strong. One possible reason is that the external costs of favors sold may be quite large. Politicians may get $1 billion in exchange for favors worth $2 to $3 bil-lion to donors, but those favors might create economic inefficiencies that cost the society hundreds of billions, even trillions of dollars worth of growth or so-cial welfare. For example, the favors sold to one industry may mean that we invest less in activities that have extremely high social benefits. If a utility gives politicians $50,000 for lower regulations worth $100,000 to the utility, it is possible that the pollution caused by lower levels of regulation will have social consequences well in excess of the private benefits realized by the utilities. Of course, these actions might also have social benefits. Ultimately, the possibility of such external effects should be mitigated by a well-functioning system of representation, in which a critical media and other democratic institutions expose the external costs of the campaign contributions, and voters will punish politicians. We are unsure how to gauge the value of such externalities, and few critics of campaign finance actually make this argument. It seems unlikely that such external costs if real could be attributed to the campaign finance system. Removing all of the favors sold from the federal budget would affect the budget only slightly. If money is not channeled to worthy public goods, it is likely for other reasons.

Another explanation of perception that corruption is of growing concern, and one we find more convincing, is that this perception confounds the politician's problem with the society's problem. Journalistic accounts such as Birnbaum's (2000) describe life in Washington, and money's corrupting influence on it. They portray the struggles of individual politicians who come to D.C. embracing ideal views of public life and end up compromising their ideals and values to gain political power. As money has grown in D.C., it has, more and more, become the means to power.

Such descriptions of life inside the beltway capture a growing *political* problem, not a growing social or policy problem. Taking the vantage of those inside the beltway, interest group politics probably do look a lot more corrupt than they did in 1980 for exactly the reasons pointed to in this paper. Favor selling, to the extent that it is the underpinning of campaign fund raising, has grown with the size of the economy. The size of the Congress, however, has not increased. On a per legislator basis deal making and favor selling, then, must be on the rise. From the perspective of the voter, steady growth in favor selling makes insider politics indeed look more corrupt, because each politician must engage in more activities that at least have the flavor of corrupt practices.

Eventually, the political problem may become an acute one. Congress may reform campaign finance simply to rekindle trust in the institution. However, the social costs associated with those political problems are not felt acutely by the typical voter because the economic costs of campaign contributions are small and remain in check. Most voters, thus, favor campaign finance reform, though it is an issue embraced by few voters as "most important."

References

Ansolabehere, Stephen, Alan S. Gerber, and James M. Snyder, Jr. 1999. "How Campaigns Respond to Media Prices: A Study of Campaign Spending and Broadcast Advertising Prices in U.S. House Elections, 1970–1972 and 1990–1992." Unpublished manuscript.

Birnbaum, Jeffrey. 2000. *The Money Men.* New York: Times Books.

Helpman, Elhanan, and Torsten Persson. 1998. "Lobbying and Legislative Bargaining." Unpublished manuscript.

McChesney, Fred S. 1997. *Money for Nothing.* Cambridge, Mass.: Harvard University Press.

Overacker, Lousie. 1932. *Money in Elections.* New York: The Macmillan Company.

Sorauf, Frank J. 1992. *Inside Campaign Finance.* New Haven: Yale University Press.

Tullock, Gordon. 1972. "The Purchase of Politicians." *Western Economic Journal* 10: 354–55.

———. 1967. "The Welfare Costs of Tariffs, Monopoly, and Theft." *Western Economic Journal* 5: 224–32.

Verba, Sidney, Kay Lehman Schlozman, and Henry E. Brady. 1995. *Voice and Equality.* Cambridge, Mass.: Harvard University Press.

Chapter 3

Public Attitudes on Campaign Finance

William G. Mayer

While press coverage of campaign finance seems to suggest that a popular consensus has formed on the subject, a closer look at poll data reveals a more complex and conflicted response. For example, while polling data indicates that the public is remarkably cynical about the current campaign finance system and the general role that money plays in American elections, it also shows that the public is not particularly knowledgeable about how current campaign finance laws work. The public strongly supports limits—of just about any kind—on campaign contributions and spending, but is, at the same time, quite ambivalent about or opposed to proposals for public financing. And despite the efforts of reformers to create the impression of a mandate for change, most Americans, whatever their preferences as to specific reforms, don't seem very concerned about campaign finance and are skeptical about the political prospects of reform and its likely consequences.

Let's take these six points one by one and examine the polling data.

1. **The public is remarkably cynical about the current campaign finance system and the general role that money plays in American elections.** The survey evidence on this point is plentiful, as the highlights in Table 3.1 indicate. Overwhelming majorities of the American public believe that "special-interest groups have more influence than voters"; that elected officials in Washington "are mostly influenced by the pressure they receive . . . from major campaign contributors"; and that "many public officials make or change policy decisions as

a direct result of money they receive from major campaign contributors." In a series of Roper polls going back to 1973, 20 percent of the respondents have consistently claimed that "most" business corporations make "illegal contributions to political campaigns," while another 35–40 percent say that "fairly many" corporations behave this way.

The result, not surprisingly, is that Americans also express considerable dissatisfaction about the operation of current campaign finance laws. In October 1999, for example, 20 percent of a Gallup sample said that the "way federal campaigns are financed" needed to be "completely overhauled," while another 44 percent endorsed "major changes." By contrast, only 26 percent said that just "minor changes" were necessary, and only eight percent said the system was "basically fine the way it is." A 1997 CBS/New York Times survey presented a slightly different set of options and found that 35 percent of respondents believed the U.S. campaign finance system had to be "completely rebuilt," 50 percent endorsed "fundamental changes," but only eight percent said that system "works pretty well" and that "only minor changes are necessary." Shortly after the 1996 elections, Gallup asked one of its samples to evaluate seven aspects of the election. "Campaign finance laws" ranked second to last, just ahead of "political advertisements." Only seven percent were "very satisfied" with the laws, while 36 percent were "very dissatisfied."

Table 3.1. General Attitudes about Campaign Finance and the Role of Money in Elections

1. BLACK/HARRIS: "Do you agree or disagree with the following statements":

	% who agree			
	May 1992	May 1993	March 1996	Feb 1997
"Special-interest groups have more influence than voters"	83%	84%	79%	83%
"Congress is largely owned by special-interest groups"	74%	74%	74%	76%

2. GALLUP: "Which do you agree with more—elected officials in Washington are most influenced by what is in the best interests of the country, or elected officials in Washington are mostly influenced by the pressure they receive on issues from major campaign contributors?"

	Oct. 1997
Best interests of country	19%
Pressure from contributors	77%
Other/neither/don't know	4%

3.   CBS/*NYT:* "In general, do you think MANY public officials make or change policy decisions as a direct result of money they receive from major campaign contributors?"

	April 1997
Yes	75%
No	14%
Don't know	11%

4.   GALLUP: "Now we want to know the extent to which you think campaign contributions influence the policies supported by election officials. Would you say they influence elected officials a great deal, a moderate amount, not much, or not at all?"

	Jan.-Feb. 1997
Great deal	53%
Moderate amount	33%
Not much	8%
Not at all	3%
Don't know	3%

5.   ROPER: "There is increasing talk these days about the ethical and moral standards in our society. We'd like to know how widespread you think certain questionable practices are. . . . Business corporations making illegal contributions to political campaigns. Do you think that is true of most, fairly many, not too many, or very few business corporations?"

	Nov. 1973	March 1978	March 1982	March 1986	Oct. 1988	Oct. 1993
Most	21%	20%	23%	23%	15%	20%
Fairly many	36%	38%	40%	37%	34%	37%
Not too many	19%	20%	22%	21%	27%	23%
Very few	12%	8%	6%	6%	8%	7%
Don't know	12%	14%	10%	13%	17%	13%

6.   GALLUP: "Which do you agree with more—elections are generally for sale to the candidate who can raise the most money, or elections are generally won on the basis of who is the best candidate?"

	Oct. 1997
Elections are for sale	59%
Best candidate wins	37%
Other/neither/don't know	4%

7.   GALLUP: "In general, which of the following statements best represents what you feel about the way federal campaigns are financed: it needs to be completely overhauled, it needs major changes, it needs minor changes, or it is basically fine the way it is?"

	Jan.-Feb. 1997	Oct. 1999
Completely overhauled	35%	20%
Major changes	35%	44%
Minor changes	21%	26%
Fine as it is	55%	8%
Don't know	4%	2%

8.   CBS/*NYT*: "Which of the following three statements comes closest to expressing your overall view of the way political campaigns are funded in the United States: (1) On the whole, the system for funding political campaigns works pretty well and only minor changes are necessary to make it work better, or (2) There are some good things in the system for funding political campaigns but fundamental changes are needed, or (3) The system for funding political campaigns has so much wrong with it that we need to completely rebuild it."

	April 1997
Only minor changes	8%
Fundamental changes	50%
Completely rebuild it	39%
Don't know	3%

9.   GALLUP: "We'd like to know how you felt about various aspects of the election this year. Please say whether you were very satisfied, somewhat satisfied, somewhat dissatisfied, or very dissatisfied with each of the following . . . The campaign finance laws which govern the way the candidates and political parties raise money."

	Nov. 1996
Very satisfied	7%
Somewhat satisfied	26%
Somewhat dissatisfied	22%
Very dissatisfied	36%
Don't know	9%

2. The public is not particularly knowledgeable about how current campaign finance laws work. This finding should not surprise anyone familiar with the general body of work on knowledge levels within the mass public compiled by professional and academic pollsters over the last 50 years. Most Americans don't know the name of their congressman, the three branches of government, or what the Bill of Rights is. Against that background, it would be most unlikely that they were well acquainted with the details of the Federal Election Campaign Act and its numerous amendments (see Table 3.2).

Still, many Americans do have some sense of the general parameters of the system. They are aware that there are limits on contributions, but only a distinct minority know (or can guess) what the limits are and to whom they apply. Most significantly, perhaps, there is no obvious sign in these questions that one side of the campaign finance debate would clearly benefit from a better-informed public. If the public consistently overestimated the stringency of current laws, for example, one might be able to argue that the public would become even more outraged if they knew the sort of things that the laws permit. But the questions in Table 3.2 provide no evidence of this: depending on the topic and how the question is worded, survey respondents were just as likely to think the laws were less strict than they are as to err in the other direction.

Table 3.2. Public Knowledge of Current Campaign Finance Laws

1. PRINCETON SURVEY RESEARCH ASSOCIATES (April 1997): "As far as you know, how much money does current law allow _____: as much as they want, only a limited amount, or are they not allowed to contribute any money?"

A. "Private citizens to give to national political parties, for 'party-building activities' such as get-out-the-vote efforts"

As much as they want (correct)	32%
Limited amount	27%
Not allowed to contribute	1%
Don't know	40%

B. "Private citizens to give directly to the campaigns of candidates for president and Congress"

As much as they want	27%
Limited amount (correct)	41%
Not allowed to contribute	2%
Don't know	30%

C. "Corporations to give directly to the campaigns of candidates for president and Congress"

As much as they want	17%
Limited amount	43%
Not allowed to contribute (correct)	4%
Don't know	40%

D. "Corporations to give to national political parties, for 'party-building activities' such as get-out-the-vote efforts"

As much as they want (correct)	24%
Limited amount	32%
Not allowed to contribute	2%
Don't know	42%

2. *WASHINGTON POST* (Jan. 1997): "May individuals give as much as they want to the campaign of a candidate running for President or Congress, or is there a limit on how much they can contribute?"

No limit	34%
There is a limit	61%
Don't know	5%

[If respondent said in the preceding question that there was a limit] "Do you happen to know how much they [individuals] are allowed to give [to the campaign of a candidate running for President or Congress]"?

Up to $500	2%
$1,000 (correct)	10%
$1,001–2,000	2%
$2,001–5,000	3%
$10,000–25,000	4%
More than $25,000	5%

Think there is a limit but　　　　34%
don't know what it is
Don't think there is a limit　　　　39%
or don't know

3.　CBS/*NYT*(April 1997): "Just your best guess, under current campaign finance laws, what is the dollar limit that any one individual can contribute to a presidential candidate's campaign—fifty dollars, one hundred dollars, five hundred, one thousand, two thousand, or more than two thousand dollars?"

$50	16%
$100	7%
$500	10%
$1,000 (correct)	22%
$2,000	8%
More than $2,000	19%
Don't know	18%

3.　The public strongly supports limits—of just about any kind—on campaign contributions and spending. In 1997, the Gallup Poll asked respondents to evaluate six different proposals to limit spending or contributions. As shown in Table 3.3, a majority of the public endorsed every proposal, in most cases by margins of 70 percent or greater. As the other questions in the table indicate, large majorities also support reducing the contribution limit for political action committees, tightening the restrictions on the use of labor union funds for campaign purposes, and eliminating the so-called soft money exemption from the campaign finance laws (i.e., extending to the political parties the provisions that currently apply to candidates). The final three questions in Table 3.3 deal with the libertarians' favorite prescription for campaign finance: entirely eliminating contribution limits. Not surprisingly, given the data just discussed, there is strikingly little support for such a proposal. Even the most favorable of the three questions finds the public rejecting the idea by a 36 to 62 percent margin.

One objection that might be raised to the questions in Table 3.3 is that they merely ask the respondents if they support limits on spending or contributions, without offering an explicit counter-argument or hinting at the values that must be balanced against such limitations. Hence the questions in Table 3.4, which ask respondents in various ways about the tradeoff between regulating campaign finance and protecting free speech. To say the least, the American public is not especially sympathetic to the notion that campaign contributions and spending fall under the aegis of the First Amendment. In July 1997, for example, the Hart and Teeter survey offered respondents a choice between two positions: "campaign spending and contributions are forms of speech protected by the First Amendment"; and "spending and contributions have nothing to do with free speech." Fully 74 percent endorsed the latter position, while just 18 percent chose the first option. Three months later, the Gallup poll asked respondents what was more important to them: "protecting the freedom of individuals" to support candidates and parties; or "protecting government from excessive influence by campaign contributors." Though this way of posing the issue is somewhat more sympathetic to the free speech side, the sample still came down strongly in favor of "protecting government," 56 percent to 39 percent.

A CBS/*New York Times* survey tried to get at the matter in a slightly different way. First, respondents were asked if they favored or opposed reducing the contribution limits for political action committees. Then, those who favored were told that "the Supreme Court has ruled that giving campaign contributions is the same as free speech and for the most part, cannot be regulated," and asked if knowing this information changed their opinion. By and large, it did not. Even when it was strongly suggested (wrongly) that contribution limits are unconstitutional, 56 percent of the public endorsed them.

So what does the public think about amending the Constitution to permit greater limitation of campaign spending? I have been able to locate only one question on this topic, on a January 1997, Washington Post survey. On that occasion, 59 percent of the respondents favored the amendment, 38 percent were opposed.

Table 3.3. Public Attitudes about Contribution and Spending Limits

1. GALLUP (Jan.-Feb. 1997): "Please say whether you would favor or oppose the following changes in federal campaign finance laws:"

	Favor	Oppose	Don't Know
"Limiting the amount of money a candidate for federal office, such as president and Congress, can contribute to his or her own political campaign"	67%	30%	3%
"Prohibiting all noncitizens, even if they are legal residents of the United States, from contributing to political campaigns"	55%	41%	4%
"Limiting the amount of money individual citizens can contribute to the national political parties"	71%	26%	3%

"Limiting the total amount of money labor unions can contribute to U.S. House and Senate campaigns each election"	76%	20%	4%
"Limiting the total amount of money business and industry can contribute to U.S. House and Senate campaigns each election"	81%	16%	3%
"Putting a limit on the amount of money candidates for the U.S. House and Senate can raise and spend on their political campaigns"	79%	19%	2%

2. CBS/*NYT:* "In order to reduce the influence of political action committees, would you favor or oppose reducing the limit on their contributions from five thousand to one thousand dollars?"

	April 1997
Favor	70%
Oppose	21%
Don't know	9%

3. GALLUP: "I have a question about the practice by labor unions of using some of the money they collect from workers' dues to support political candidates and parties. Which of the following approaches for handling this do you favor— unions should be able to spend money from workers' dues for political purposes, unless individual workers make a special request that their dues not be used this way; or unions should be required to get permission in writing from each worker prior to spending that worker's dues for political purposes?"

	Oct. 1997
Should be able to spend dues	24%
Should get permission	72%
Neither/other/don't know	4%

4. *L.A. TIMES:* "As you may know, candidates running for national elected offices, such as President and Congress, have campaign laws restricting how much money they may receive from individual donors or political action groups, also known as PACs. However, the Democratic and Republican Parties do not have restrictions, and they may raise large sums of money from donors because the money is not raised with any one candidate in mind. The political parties can then distribute the money any way they see fit. As part of the campaign finance reform,

should the campaign finance system be changed to reduce the role of big money
that is given to candidates by political parties, or not?"

	Sept. 1997
Change	78%
Don't change	15%
Don't know	7%

5.   GALLUP: "As you may know, the federal government now limits the amount
of money that individual Americans can donate to political candidates, but the law
allows people to donate as much money as they want to political parties for general
political activities. Do you think the campaign finance laws should limit the
amount of money that people can donate both to political parties and to individual
candidates, or do you think they should only limit the amount of money that
people can donate to individual candidates?"

	Oct. 1997
Limit to both parties	63%
and candidates	
Only limit to candidates	24%
Other/neither/don't know	13%

6.   ABC/*WASHINGTON POST:* "As you may know, federal law limits the
amount of money people can contribute to any presidential candidate's campaign,
but people can give as much money as they want to any political party. Do you
think the amount of money people can contribute to political parties should be
limited, or unlimited?"

	Oct. 1999	Dec. 1999
Limited	63%	68%
Unlimited	33%	30%
Don't know	4%	1%

7.   GALLUP: "Next, I'm going to read a few proposals for changing the way
political campaigns are financed. For each one, please say whether you think that
change would make campaign financing better or not. . . . Dropping all
restrictions on the amount any individual or group can contribute to a presidential
or congressional candidate so that they could contribute as much as they want?"

	March 1997
Better	26%
Not better	71%
Don't know	3%

8. *WASHINGTON POST:* "Which of these statements comes closer to your own opinion? . . . We should put limits on the amount of money people can give to political candidates, so that everyone would have a more equal chance to compete for office. People should be free to contribute as much money as they want to any political candidate they choose."

	Aug. 1998
Put limits	67%
Contribute as much as they want	30%
Neither/don't know	3%

9. CBS: "Which one of the following two positions on campaign financing do you favor more: limiting the amount of money individuals can contribute to political campaigns, or allowing individuals to contribute as much money to political campaigns as they'd like?"

	July 1999
Limiting contributions	62%
Allowing unlimited contributions	36%
Don't know	2%

Table 3.4. Public Attitudes about the Tradeoff between Protecting Free Speech and Regulating Campaign Finance

1. HART AND TEETER: "Some people say that campaign spending and contributions are forms of speech protected by the First Amendment and cannot be regulated. Other people say that campaign spending and contributions have nothing to do with free speech and that limits should be imposed. Which position do you agree with?"

	July 1997
Form of free speech	18%
Nothing to do with free speech	74%
Don't know	8%

2. GALLUP: "Thinking about any new campaign finance laws that might be passed, which of the following is more important to you—protecting the freedom of individuals to support political candidates and parties financially, or protecting government from excessive influence by campaign contributors?"

	Oct. 1997
Protecting individuals	39%
Protecting government from influence	56%
Don't know	5%

3.   HART AND TEETER: "Some people say that some campaign finance reform is needed because there is too much money being spent on political campaigns, which leads to excessive influence by special interests and wealthy individuals at the expense of average people. Others say that some campaign finance reform is not needed because the Supreme Court has ruled that campaign spending is protected as free speech and people should not be limited in their participation in the political process. Which of these statements comes closer to your point of view?"

	Sept. 1997
Need reform to limit special interests	77%
Shouldn't limit participation	18%
Don't know	5%

4.   CBS/*NYT* (April 1997): "In order to reduce the influence of political action committees, would you favor or oppose reducing the limit on their contributions from five to one thousand dollars? [IF FAVOR] As you may know, the Supreme Court has ruled that giving campaign contributions is the same as free speech and for the most part, cannot be regulated. Given that, would you favor or oppose reducing the limit on political action committees' contributions from five thousand to one thousand dollars?"

	Response to Initial Question		Response to Second Question
Favor	70%	Favor	56%
Oppose	21%	Oppose[a]	31%
Don't know	9%	Don't know[a]	13%

[a]"Oppose" and "don't know" percentages include those who gave these responses to the initial question, and were therefore never asked the follow up question.

5.   *WASHINGTON POST:* "As you may know, the U.S. Supreme Court has defined political advertising as a form of free speech that cannot currently be restricted under the Constitution. Would you favor or oppose a constitutional amendment to place limits on these kinds of contributions?"

Public Attitudes on Campaign Finance

Jan. 1997

Favor	59%
Oppose	38%
Don't know	3%

4. The public is quite ambivalent about or opposed to proposals for public financing of election campaigns. Public financing is the sort of issue, quite common in survey research, where what public opinion looks like depends a great deal on the way the survey questions are worded. A reasonably representative sample of such questions is shown in Table 3.5, ranked according to the percentage that favor public financing. That percentage varies between 18 percent and 52 percent; opposition runs from 78 percent to 36 percent. Still, if there is a central tendency to these results, it clearly seems to fall on the side of opposition to public financing. Indeed, only one of the eight questions in Table 3.5 finds a majority of the American public in favor of public financing, while five register majorities in opposition.

Table 3.5. Public Opinion about Public Financing of Election Campaigns

1. CBS/*NYT*: "Some people have proposed public financing of political campaigns—that is, using ONLY tax money to pay for political campaigns. Would you favor or oppose public financing to pay for political campaigns?"

	April 1997
Favor public financing	18%
Oppose public financing	78%
Don't know	4%

2. CIVIC SERVICE: "It has been proposed in Congress that the federal government provide public financing for congressional campaigns for the House of Representatives and Senate. Would you approve or disapprove of the proposal to use public funds, federal money, to pay the costs of congressional campaigns, and how strongly do you feel?"

	1985	1986
Favor public financing	27%	21%
Oppose public financing	65%	71%
Don't know	8%	8%

3. GALLUP: "Next, 'I'm going to read a few proposals for changing the way political campaigns are financed. For each one, please say whether you think that change would make campaign financing better or not. . . . Establishing federal

financing of presidential and congressional campaigns in which all Americans would be required to pay some additional taxes, and candidates would agree to federal restrictions on the amount of money they could spend?"

	March 1997
Better	35%
Not better	60%
Don't know	5%

4.   NBC/*WSJ:* "Do you favor or oppose making funds available to finance campaigns for Congress, in exchange for limits on campaign contributions from individuals and political action committees?"

	Dec. 1990	Apr. 1993
Favor public financing	38%	38%
Oppose public financing	55%	53%
Don't know	7%	9%

5.   GALLUP: "Please say whether you would favor or oppose the following changes in federal campaign finance laws. . . . Establishing a new campaign finance system where federal campaigns are funded by the government and all contributions from individuals and private groups are banned?"

	Jan.-Feb. 1997
Favor public financing	43%
Oppose public financing	52%
Don't know	5%

6.   CBS: "In order to reduce congressional campaign contributions from special interests, would you favor or oppose public financing to help congressional candidates in their campaigns?"

	March 1997
Favor	43%
Oppose	46%
Don't know	11%

7.   HART AND TEETER: "Would you favor or oppose a plan that prohibits all political contributions from corporations, unions, special interests, and individuals, and instead funds all political campaigns from the federal treasury?"

	March 1997
Favor	46%
Oppose	42%
Don't know	12%

8.   GALLUP: "It has been suggested that the federal government provide a fixed amount of money for the election campaigns of candidates for Congress and that all private contributions be prohibited. Do you think this is a good idea or a poor idea?"

	July 1984	March 1987
Favor public financing	52%	50%
Oppose public financing	36%	42%
Don't know	12%	8%

5.   Whatever their preferences as to specific reforms, most Americans don't seem very concerned about campaign finance. I was, frankly, surprised how strong the evidence is on this point. One can find survey questions that might seem to endorse the opposite conclusion. There are what I will call "absolute priority questions": questions that ask respondents to assess campaign finance reform in isolation or whether campaign finance issues matter to them. A small sample of such questions is shown in Table 3.6. In an ABC/*Washington Post* poll, for example, 44 percent of an October 1997, sample said that reforming campaign finance laws should be "a major goal" of the federal government. In the same month, Gallup found 16 percent of respondents said that campaign finance reform should be "the top priority" for Congress and the president in the next year, while another 32 percent said it should be "a high priority." In April of this year, 34 percent of the public said campaign finance would be "very important" in determining how they vote in the 2000 presidential election.

After examining a succession of such questions on a variety of topics, it is apparent that questions of this type set a very undemanding standard for the survey respondent. What, after all, does it really mean to say that an issue is "very important" or "a top priority"? Certainly the question does not require any actual demonstration of concern or commitment. A far better way to assess such matters is to look at the relative ranking of an issue: how it compares to the numerous other items that are likely to be on the public agenda at any one time.

Table 3.7 presents a collection of these "relative priority" questions, and as I have already suggested, it is striking how low campaign finance rates as a public concern. In January 2000, for example, the Gallup poll asked a national sample of Americans how important 25 different issues would be "when you vote in this year's presidential election." "Campaign finance reform" ranked 24th on the list; the only issue most Americans found less pressing was "policy concerning gays and lesbians." In 1997, a CBS/*New York Times* poll presented respondents with

62   *William G. Mayer*

a list of four problems-"ensuring a healthy economy," "creating better schools," "reforming campaign finance laws," and "reducing crime"—and asked which was "most important right now." Campaign finance ranked dead last, well behind the other three.

In a 1994 exit poll, Mitofsky International listed nine issues and asked those who just voted, "Which two issues mattered most in deciding how you voted for U.S. House?" "Campaign finance reform" ranked next to last, one percentage point ahead of "foreign trade/NAFTA." (In other years, campaign finance has not been among the specific issues listed on exit poll ballots.) One of the standard questions in the Harris Survey asks, "What do you think are the two most important issues for the government to address?" Throughout 1997 and 1998, the number answering "campaign finance" hovered at around one percent and never exceeded three percent.

Table 3.6. Public Attitudes about Campaign Finance as an Absolute Priority

1. ABC/*WASHINGTON POST:* "I'm going to mention a few things the federal government could try to accomplish. For each one, please tell me whether you think it should or should not be a goal for government to accomplish. . . . Reforming election campaign finance laws . . . should it be a major goal or a minor goal for government?"

	Oct. 1997
Major goal	44%
Minor goal	39%
Not a goal (vol.)	14%
Don't know	3%

2. GALLUP: "Here are some issues now being discussed in Washington. For each one, please tell me whether you think it should be the top priority for Congress and the President to deal with in the next year, a high priority, a low priority, or not a priority at all. How high a priority should be given to . . . campaign finance reform?"

	Oct. 1997
Top priority	16%
High	32%
Low	39%
Not a priority	10%
Don't know	4%

3. OPINION DYNAMICS: "How strongly do you personally feel about the need for campaign finance reform?"

	Oct. 1997
Very strongly	44%
Somewhat strongly	24%
Not too strongly	13%
Not strongly at all	11%
Don't know	8%

4. PRINCETON SURVEY RESEARCH ASSOCIATES: "Thinking ahead to the November [1998] election for Congress in your district, how much of a factor will each of the following issues be in deciding which candidate you'll vote for. Will a candidate's position on . . . campaign finance reform—be the most important factor in your decision, one of many factors you'll consider, or not a factor?"

	Aug. 1997
Most important factor	15%
One of many factors	45%
Not a factor	33%
Don't plan to vote (vol.)	3%
Don't know	4%

5. ABC/*WASHINGTON POST:* "How important will . . . reforming election campaign finance laws . . . be to you in deciding how to vote in the 2000 presidential election in November—very important, somewhat important, not too important, or not important at all?"

	March-Apr. 2000
Very important	34%
Somewhat important	36%
Not too important	16%
Not important at all	11%
Don't know	3%

Table 3.7. Public Attitudes about Campaign Finance as a Relative Priority

1. GALLUP (Jan. 2000): "Next, we'd like to know which issues will be important to you when you vote in this year's presidential election. As I read each issue, please tell me if it will be extremely important to your vote, very important, somewhat important, not too important, or not important at all."

	Extremely	Very	Some what	Not Too	Not at all	Average Ranking
Public education	39	46	11	2	1	4.21
Cost of healthcare	32	49	16	2	0	4.12
Soc. Sec. and Medicare for future generations	31	51	14	2	1	4.10
Current policy on Soc. Sec. and Medicare	29	50	18	3	0	4.05
Nation's economy	28	53	16	2	0	4.08
Raising children	33	44	16	4	2	4.03
Lack of health insurance	31	42	21	4	1	3.99
Presidential character	29	45	19	4	2	3.96
Amount paid in fed. taxes	29	43	21	5	1	3.95
Poverty and homelessness	26	46	23	3	1	3.94
Federal income tax system	25	45	24	4	1	3.90
Budget surplus	24	44	24	4	1	3.89
Moral standards	29	42	18	7	3	3.88
Medical care in HMOs	26	43	22	5	2	3.88
Crime prevention	23	48	22	5	1	3.88
The environment	23	45	34	5	2	3.75
Gun laws	25	38	24	8	4	3.73
US role in world affairs	17	43	30	6	2	3.68
Military spending	18	38	32	9	2	3.62
Race relations	20	36	29	7	6	3.58
Power of federal gov't	17	36	32	9	4	3.54
Foreign trade	10	34	41	10	3	3.39
Abortion policy	19	28	26	15	11	3.29
Campaign finance reform	12	22	37	18	8	3.12
Policy concerning gays and lesbians	8	17	30	21	22	2.67

2.   CBS/*NYT:* "Which of these four problems do you think is most important right now—ensuring a healthy economy, creating better schools, reforming campaign finance laws, or reducing crime?"

	April 1997
Reducing crime	42%
Creating better schools	32%
Ensuring healthy economy	19%
Reforming campaign finance	4%
Don't know	2%

3.   MARKET STRATEGIES: "There has been a lot of talk about reform in Washington. Which of the following do you, personally, think is the most important to address right now: federal tax reform, health care reform, campaign finance reform, social security?"

	June 1998
Health care reform	33%
Social security	27%
Federal tax reform	26%
Campaign finance reform	7%
All equal (vol.)	6%
Don't know	1%

4.   ROPER (March 1991): "Here are some things people have said Congress should be working on. [Card shown to respondent.] Obviously, one Congressman or one Senator can give major attention to only a limited number of problems. I'd like you to tell me for each of those things whether it is something you'd like to see your Congressperson or Senator give major attention to, or whether you would rather have him or her devote attention to more important things?"

	Give Major Attention	Devote to More Important Things	Don't Know
"A program to provide national health insurance for everyone"	73%	21%	5%
"The development of a national energy policy"	64%	28%	8%
"Stricter regulations on the way dangerous chemicals can be transported from one place in the country to another"	64%	28%	8%
"Tax reform"	63%	28%	10%
"A program to reform the banking system"	49%	40%	11%
"Eliminating discrimination in the workplace"	48%	45%	7%
"Stricter labeling regulations for food products"	42%	50%	8%
"Reform of our campaign finance laws"	36%	52%	12%

5. MITOFSKY INTERNATIONAL (self-administered exit poll): "Which 2 Issues Mattered Most In Deciding How You Voted For U.S. House?"

	Nov. 1994
Crime	35%
Economy/jobs	27%
Taxes	23%
Health care	21%
Family values/morality	21%
Education	18%
Abortion	13%
Campaign finance reform	4%
Foreign trade/NAFTA	3%

6. HARRIS: "What do you think are the two most important issues for the government to address?"

	Percent mentioning "campaign finance"
May 1997	1%
Oct. 1997	3%
Jan. 1998	1%
Aug. 1998	1%
Sept. 1998	*%
Oct. 1998	*%
Nov. 1998	*%
* = Less than 0.5%	

6. Americans seem skeptical about the political prospects of reform and its likely consequences. Why is campaign finance such an obscure blip on the national radar screen? Certainly one cannot claim that the media refuse to cover the issue. Part of the answer may be that, unlike issues such as education, unemployment, and taxes, problems with the campaign finance system do not seem to have an immediate, direct impact on the lives of most Americans. To be sure, those who advocate a wholesale restructuring of the campaign finance laws often argue that reforms in these other areas will occur only if the role of money in American elections is greatly diminished: that changes in the campaign finance laws are an important precondition for adopting national health insurance or an equitable tax code. To judge from the data in Table 3.7, that argument has yet to catch on.

Another reason for the public's lack of interest in campaign finance may be that the most zealous proponents of change have been, in a sense, too successful in propagating their basic world view. If money so completely dominates

American politics, if everything is for sale, if both parties are thoroughly corrupt, then it is difficult to explain how new laws would make much difference or who could assemble the kind of political coalition necessary to enact them.

In fact, Americans are quite skeptical on both of these points. On the one hand, they see very little difference between the parties in terms of their past record on campaign finance or their commitment to future reforms. Though Democratic party practices have received the most investigation and criticism over the last several years, the public clearly believed Republicans were not very different (see Table 3.8).

Equally important, many Americans express considerable skepticism as to whether changing the campaign finance laws will really "level the playing field" to any significant degree. As the questions in Table 3.9 indicate, a plurality of the American public apparently believe that, even if the campaign finance system were substantially overhauled, nothing fundamental would change. Money would still find a way to make its influence felt, "special interests" would still rule the roost. In 1998, for example, the Gallup poll offered its respondents a choice between two positions: "major changes to the laws governing campaign finance could succeed in reducing the power of special interests"; and "no matter what new laws are passed, special interests will always find a way to maintain their power." Just 31 percent chose the first statement, while 63 percent endorsed the second.

Table 3.8. Comparisons of Democratic and Republican Party Fundraising Practices

1. HARRIS: "Which political party—the Republicans or Democrats—do you think are more influenced by the interests of those who give money to their campaigns, or is there no difference?"

	March 1997
Republicans more influenced	17%
Democrats more influenced	14%
No difference	67%
Don't know	2%

2. GALLUP: "If you believe that either political party's campaign fundraising in 1996 was unethical, which party's fundraising do you think was more unethical—the Republican party's, the Democratic party's, or were they about the same?"

	Jan.-Feb. 1997
Republican party	9%
Democratic party	19%
About the same	67%

Neither party unethical (vol.)   1%
Don't know   4%

3. CBS/*NYT:* "In general, do you think the campaign fundraising practices the Democrats used in 1996 are common practices that both political parties use, or are they practices that only the Democrats have used?"

	April 1997
Done by both parties	77%
Only the Democrats	13%
Don't know	10%

Table 3.9.   Public Attitudes about the Effectiveness of Campaign Finance Reform

1. GALLUP (March 1998): "Some people say major changes to the laws governing campaign finance could succeed in reducing the power of special interests in Washington. Other people say no matter what new laws are passed, special interests will always find a way to maintain their power in Washington. Which comes closer to your point of view?"

Major changes would reduce power of special interests	31%
Special interests will maintain power	63%
Neither/other/don't know	6%

2. HART AND TEETER: "Suppose that Congress passed campaign finance reform legislation. Some people say that campaign finance reform would have a positive effect on the political system, because it would reduce the influence that the wealthy and special interests have on elections. Other people say that campaign finance reform would have no effect on the political system, because the wealthy and special interests will always find loopholes in the law and continue to have just as much influence on elections. Which point of view do you agree with more? If you do not know or are not sure, please just say so."

	Oct. 1999	Jan. 2000
Would have positive effect	43%	40%
Would have no effect	44%	47%
Don't know	13%	11%

In closing, let me mention a few issues that I have not dealt with here, and that a more complete examination of this topic probably ought to include.

1. The demographics of mass opinion. So far as I can determine, not a single published book or article goes beyond the kind of survey marginals that have been the focus of this paper, and looks at how such attitudes are distributed across major population subgroups. Who supports public financing? Who opposes it? Two variables that do not seem to matter much are party and ideology. At the elite level, advocates of public financing tend to be largely Democrats and liberals—but there is little evidence of the same sort of clustering at the level of mass opinion.

2. Attitudes about state campaign finance laws. All of the survey questions examined in this paper are drawn from national opinion polls and deal with federal laws and elections. But some of the most interesting and innovative work on campaign finance issues today is being done at the state level. In most respects, I suspect that survey data on state campaign finance practices will have the same general outline as the questions on federal campaign financing. Most Americans are cynical about government at every level and probably think that money also dominates state and local elections. But it would be interesting to see if there is good survey data available from states that have experimented with public financing systems, to see whether they have made residents noticeably less cynical or less alienated.

Chapter 4

Hey, Wait a Minute:
The Assumptions Behind the Case for Campaign Finance Reform

Kenneth R. Mayer

One of the persistent mysteries of campaign finance reform is why the public doesn't seem to care much about it. Despite clear evidence that an overwhelming majority of voters thinks that the whole financing system is utterly broken, there is almost no evidence that they care one way or another about where candidates stand on the issue, and nothing to suggest that any federal candidates have won or lost because of their position on reform.[1] Efforts to connect campaign contributions to major public policy decisions—free trade, airline regulation, energy policy, taxes, bankruptcy reform—get no traction. Not even a major scandal—the 1996 controversy over foreign soft money contributions or

---

[1]In a November 2000 poll conducted by the Pew Center for People and the Press, respondents who said that their support for either Bush or Gore stemmed largely from the candidates' issue positions were asked *which* issues were most important in that determination. Campaign finance reform was mentioned by less than one percent; the top issue was education, at 28 percent (http://www.people-press.org/loct00que.htm). A March 2001 Fox News poll asked respondents to identify the most important problem facing the nation. Taxes were first, named by 31 percent of respondents; education was second, at 29 percent. Campaign finance was tied for 18th place, named by one percent of respondents.

Clinton's last minute pardon of fugitive financier Marc Rich—can produce sustainable momentum in favor of reform.

What accounts for this disconnection? One explanation is that campaign finance reform generates less salience because it is viewed as a question of process, not substance. Because campaign finance is only indirectly related to political decisions, voters care less about it than about kitchen-table issues such as education, taxes, prescription drug coverage, or the economy.

I propose an alternative explanation: inadequate media coverage of campaign finance issues and the simplistic arguments offered by many campaign finance reformers make it impossible to distinguish true corruption from the every-day pull and haul of politics. Too often, reform arguments reduce complicated political processes to a simplistic money-equals-votes relationship. In so doing, they construct explanations that fail to meet basic logical standards. The strategy is more rhetorical than logical and usually involves some variant of the following flawed syllogism:

Major Premise: Interest groups lobby and contribute money to Congress

Minor Premise: Congress makes legislative decisions

Conclusion: All legislative decisions are based solely on interest group contributions and lobbying

This argument leads naturally to the conclusion that *everything* about political decision-making is corrupt and crowds out arguments about the merits and flaws of particular legislative proposals.

My critique of the reform literature relies on the argument that it too often embodies several fallacies: first, that criticisms of campaign finance often fall back on explanations that cannot be proven wrong, no matter what the facts are; second, "selection bias" ignores cases in which campaign money *could not* have determined the outcome, or cases in which the outcome was precisely the reverse of what was expected; third, that most reform arguments invariably confuse correlation with causation; and finally, that there exists some "objective" public interest that legislators would gravitate toward if not for the corrupting influence of campaign cash. While these objections may seem like high-minded academic nitpicking, they are in fact central to crafting a realistic picture of what, precisely, is the problem.

Getting it Wrong

At times, media reports on the influence of campaign contributions are simply wrong. In its February 7, 2000 issue, *Time* magazine ran an article on an obscure provision of an obscure appropriations bill hustled through Congress at the last minute. Investigative reporters Donald Bartlett and James Steele noted that in language buried deep within the fiscal year 2000 District of Columbia appropriations act, Congress gave scrap recyclers an exemption for any liability under the Superfund environmental cleanup program. The provision, in English, meant that scrap recyclers could not be sued for the costs of cleaning up Superfund toxic sites, even if materials they processed had contributed to polluted landfills. The scrap industry argued that this exemption—for which they had lobbied for years—was necessary to encourage recycling and to fix an unintended consequence of the Superfund law.[2]

To Bartlett and Steele, "it was just your typical piece of Congressional dirty work" resulting from nothing more than well-placed campaign contributions.[3] In return for $300,000 in donations in the 1990s, they concluded, Congress let scrap dealers "off the hook for millions of dollars in potential Superfund liabilities at toxic-waste sites." It seemed to be a textbook consequence of a corrupt campaign finance system, in which narrow interest groups obtained a special political favor at the expense of the public welfare; just another case of the public getting shafted by fat-cat corporate plutocrats and their big money lobbyists.

Except that isn't what happened. It was, in fact, a case where a campaign-finance David actually slew Goliath: the proverbial "little guy" won. Bartlett and Steele fundamentally misread the role that special interests played in the debate over the Superfund Equity Recycling Act, and dramatically overstated the effect that campaign contributions had on the final outcome. In omitting critical parts of the story, they reduced a complicated legislative process to a one-dimensional and inaccurate portrait of money corrupting legislative decision-making.

Here is the part Bartlett and Steele left out: In exempting recyclers from liability under Superfund, Congress actually shifted about $700 million in potential cleanup costs from scrap dealers to other companies in the manufacturing-disposal chain. The "millions of dollars in potential Superfund liabilities at toxic-waste sites" did not disappear and did not get foisted upon an unwitting public, but were transferred.

Not surprisingly, the companies who would *now* have to absorb the costs—including some of the largest corporations in the world, such as Dow Chemical, DuPont, General Motors, General Electric, Waste Management Inc., and Westinghouse—thought the bill was a terrible idea. The Chemical Manufacturers Association wrote to every legislator urging them to oppose the exemption. The American Insurance Association, the Business Roundtable, the National Association of Manufacturers, and an industry group called the Superfund Action Alliance wrote to legislators in November 1999 asserting that "such a cost-shift would be equivalent to a large, new hidden tax on businesses that could threaten

---

[2]The unintended consequence was that recyclers of, say, aluminum, could be liable for superfund cleanup costs incurred by a company that purchased the recycled material, whereas a supplier of so-called virgin aluminum would not be.

[3]Donald L. Bartlett and James B. Steele, "How the Little Guy Gets Crunched," *Time*, February 7, 2000.

their viability and would only make Superfund even more unfair than it is already."[4]

If campaign contributions and naked political power were the deciding factors in the law, big business should have won in a rout. Companies opposed to the recycling provision contributed tens of millions of dollars to legislators and parties during the 1990s, perhaps 200 times as much as the recyclers gave. In return, they got nothing. Yet you would never know this by reading the *Time* story. The Superfund Recycling Equity Act passed, and the beneficiaries contributed money, so the money bought the outcome. *QED.*

The main problem with this faulty reasoning is that it cannot be proven wrong. If you begin with the axiom that money drives votes, you will always be able to find evidence to support it, no matter what the outcome, no matter who wins. Consider how Bartlett and Steele might have written their story if the recycling equity act had *failed*. In that case, it would have been even easier to explain the outcome as the result of the lobbying and campaign contributions by huge corporate polluters (something along the lines of "$80 million in corporate contributions defeats legislation to make recycling easier"). A simple reversal of the names—"corporate polluters kill Superfund exemption" instead of "recyclers win Superfund exemption"—would still "prove" the point that a powerful interest group bought legislation.[5]

Indeed, this is precisely what happened in 1998 when the recycling industry tried, and failed, to get the same exemption. One account attributed the recyclers' loss to the fact that they "lacked the clout to carry the day," and concluded, "the special interests won" because of lobbying and campaign contributions by other manufacturers in the waste management chain.[6] So, the special interests "won" in 1998 when the recycling exemption failed. And the special interests "won" in 1999, when the recycling exemption passed. Congress is on the hook either way.

This pattern reflects the standard method for analyzing money in politics. The process is simple: look for a piece of legislation that confers some benefit on an interest group that has made campaign contributions and conclude that the campaign contributions produced the legislation. But following this template ensures that narratives will vastly oversimplify the complexity of political decision-making and reduce a multifaceted process to a simple, inviolable, and in-

---

[4]See Judith Jacobs, "Scrap Recycling Liability Exemption in Funding Bill Awaiting Clinton's Signature," *Environment Reporter,* November 26, 1999, 1369; "AIA Warns Against Exemptions to Superfund Legislation," *The Underwriter's Wire Report,* November 11, 1999.

[5]There is actually a separate problem: nowhere is there any discussion of whether or not the recycling exemption was good public policy.

[6]W. John Moore, "Waste Not, Win Not," *National Journal,* October 31, 1998, 2569.

controvertible correlation between campaign contributions and political outcomes.

To reformers, this isn't a problem, since the "money = votes" connection is so self-evident as to scarcely require elaboration; anyone who questions it must be either willfully ignorant or deliberately dishonest. The very existence of huge sums of money in the political process is *ipso facto* evidence of corruption. But the argument that money and outcomes are related is a far cry from the argument that money *caused* the outcome. To suggest that money does not buy votes is not to say that money has no influence at all. But it does mean that we have to recognize that things are far more complex than they are portrayed.

The Problem of Money and Votes—Three Cases

The example I offered above—the Superfund Recycling Equity Act—is a typical example of an oversimplified analysis and a nonfalsifiable explanation. No matter which way the vote went, one could—indeed, people did—attribute it to the lobbying and campaign contributions of whatever side won. But moving beyond drawing simple correlations almost invariably will produce a story that is more complex, and it is not at all difficult to find cases that "disprove" the thesis that money drives political outcomes; I offer three such cases below. My goal is not to absolve the campaign finance system of all sins; rather, it is to highlight the complexity of legislative decision-making and to emphasize the logical gaps in much of the reform literature.

Free Trade with China: Confusing Correlation with Causation

In April 2000, the House of Representatives voted 237–197 to establish permanent normal trade relations (PNTR) with China (or, more specifically, to eliminate the annual review of China's trade status). Although the legislation did not attract much public interest, it was enormously important to business (who wanted the bill passed), and labor groups (who were against it). To business, free trade with China could open the world's largest untapped market to American exports and investment. Unions, in contrast, feared that manufacturing jobs would shift to China because of its lower labor costs.

Soon after the vote, The Center for Responsive Politics (CRP), a campaign finance reform group, suggested that the vote was the result of large campaign contributions by the Business Roundtable, a coalition of large corporations that has donated nearly $60 million to candidates and parties during the 1999–2000 election cycle. The PNTR vote was, according to a center press release, "a major victory for members of the Business Roundtable, a coalition of more than 200 corporations that had pumped millions of dollars into lobbying members of Congress in favor of the legislation."[7]

The CRP based its conclusion on an analysis of the relationship between Business Roundtable contributions and the House vote. As is common in this sort of analysis, the CRP noted that the 237 House members who voted yes on PNTR received, on average, $44,000 from PACs and individuals associated with the Business Roundtable. The 197 members who voted "no" received $25,000.[8] The clear implication is that the vote was "bought." Members tallied up the money they received from the different sides, and voted based upon who gave them the most.

But one can't really infer much from the data. Any simple comparison of campaign contributions and votes fails to account for the direction of the causal relationship, something critical to any full understanding of campaign finance reform. Just by looking at campaign contributions it's simply not possible to determine whether a legislator voted in favor of PNTR because of business contributions (or against it because of labor contributions), or whether business contributions flowed to members who were *already* predisposed to favor the pro-business position (and vice-versa for labor).

Ideology more likely played a key role, because there is evidence that votes broke along traditional business-labor lines. Republicans favored the bill by nearly a 3–1 margin, while Democrats were opposed nearly 2–1. But there is clear evidence that the lines were not so sharply defined. Some decidedly liberal Democrats (Charles Rangel, Sander Levin, Henry Waxman, Sheila Jackson-Lee) voted yes along with some of the chamber's most conservative Republicans (Tom DeLay, Asa Hutchinson, Ernest Istook). You won't often find Bernie Sanders (Ind-N.H.) and Jessie Jackson, Jr. (D-Ill.) on the same side as Bob Barr (R-Ga.) and Lindsey Graham (R-S.C.). They all voted "no." It's surely a stretch to argue that you could put together such an odd coalition for or against anything based on a campaign check.

In addition to simplistically connecting contributions and votes, CRP proceeds to construct a non-falsifiable explanation of the outcome. Having concluded that votes *for* PNTR vote were because of Business Roundtable campaign money, did the CRP conclude that a vote *against* PNTR was a principled stand against corporate hegemony or a sign of support for human rights? Not a chance. "No" votes were bought by labor: "Unions," the report continued, "which have contributed roughly $31 million in soft money, PAC and individual contributions this election year, also appeared to play a significant role in how

---

[7]Center for Responsive Politics, "A Passage to China Update: House Approves PNTR," *Money in Politics Alert,* May 24, 2000.

[8]Center for Responsive Politics, "House Vote on China Trade" (http://www.opensecrets.org/news/china_housea.htm).

the House voted." House members who voted "no" received, on average, $58,000 from labor unions, while those who voted "yes" got only $23,000.

We are left with an account that insists there is only one possible explanation: the interest groups put their money into Congress, members looked at which side gave them the most, and voted accordingly. But this explanation cannot be true. Unions, in fact, contributed *more* to House members than business interests (at least those interests identified by the CRP as having the biggest stake in the vote)—$17 million to $15 million. If members based their votes simply on who gave them the most money, then labor should have won.

Did business interests have a stake in the PNTR vote? Absolutely. So did organized labor. So did the Friends of the Earth, Human Rights Watch, and Focus on the Family, for that matter. An observer would have to be willfully blind to deny that lobbying and campaign contributions were a factor in the vote. But it is equally shortsighted to suggest that money was the defining dimension.

When Money Buys Gridlock

On its face, electricity deregulation would appear to be a classic issue area in which interest groups would dominate: a complex, technical, narrow issue, where individual public stakes are small (barring, of course, a California-scale disaster), but where the overall stakes for the affected industries are huge. The key issue is whether retail electricity supply should be governed by market forces, with customers able to choose their provider (in a situation analogous to selection of long-distance phone service). Supporters of deregulation argue that it will generate lower costs and better service, since competition will reward those companies that can operate most efficiently, while opponents note the potential for ratepayers to get stuck with higher utility bills.

Because of the sector's size—electric utilities had $218 billion in retail sales in 1999—the risks were great that a powerful interest would have its way with any restructuring proposals, with the public certain to be left behind. According to the CRP, electric utilities spent over $60 million on lobbying and campaign contributions in 1997 and 1998 alone.[9] Yet despite numerous attempts, nothing has passed. If money drives votes, then surely the industry would have had its way on such an arcane issue.

But, as it turns out, electric utilities are hardly monolithic on restructuring legislation, and differences among the various subsets of utility interests have made agreement impossible. Some utility groups want the federal government to take the lead, while others want state-level action. Disputes continue over which regulatory bureaucracy will exercise oversight. Some want rapid deregulation

---

[9]Center for Responsive Politics (http://www.opensecrets.org/pubs/lobby98/topind05. htm).

with a specified deadline for action, while others want a slower approach that gives them time to adapt. Legislators have not figured out how to treat for-profit investor-owned utilities alongside nonprofit utilities (such as the Tennessee Valley Authority). These differences have produced multiple legislative approaches, none of which has been able to muster broad support; the Department of Energy identified 31 different utility restructuring bills in the 106th Congress.[10]

No amount of campaign cash, it seems, can create consensus out of thin air. California's disastrous experience with utility deregulation is almost certain to make reform even harder to achieve.[11]

Oddly enough, Public Citizen has accused Congress of *intentionally* keeping the bill stalled, in order to maintain pressure on the power industry to contribute even more money:

> Both sides of the debate are giving Congress large amounts of money, which is why we haven't seen a bill go anywhere. . . . [That way, lawmakers] can keep the money raising going. There's no benefit to passing a bill now. . . . They have to make it appear that there's enough movement to allow the K Street crowd to keep billing their clients.[12]

It is difficult to construct an explanation for congressional behavior that would be harder to disprove than this: when Congress acts it does so because members are beholden to special interest campaign contributions; when Congress does not act it does so because members are beholden to special interest contributions.

When the "Special Interests" Lose

The reform literature creates an inaccurate impression about money's role in politics by ignoring cases where Congress votes contrary to what interested money would like.

A recent report by Common Cause criticized the influence of the alcohol and restaurant industries in defeating a 1998 effort to establish a nationwide drunk driving standard of .08 percent blood alcohol level. After noting that alcohol interests had contributed nearly $23 million to candidates and parties during the 1990s, the report notes that:

---

[10]Department of Energy, Energy Information Administration, *The Changing Structure of the Electric Power Industry 2000: An Update.* DOE/EIA-0562(00), October 2000, 55–59.

[11]James C. Benton and Chuck McCutcheon, "Electricity Deregulation Supporters, Skeptics, Draw Lessons from California Crisis," *CQ Weekly Report,* January 27, 2001.

[12]James C. Benton, "Money and Power: The Fight Over Electricity Deregulation," *CQ Weekly Report,* August 12, 2000, 1964.

the alcohol industry was joined by restaurant interests in successfully fighting off an attempt to strengthen drunk-driving standards at the national level. A measure to penalize states that failed to lower their minimum blood alcohol level from .10 to .08 by restricting federal highway funds passed in the Senate. But after intense lobbying by the alcohol industry, the measure never made it out of the House Rules Committee.[13]

At almost the same time, the Center for Responsive Politics issued a report that criticized the industry for fighting the same provision in 2000.[14]

So far, at least, the contours of this discussion parallel the congressional action on recyclers and China trade: the interested parties (alcohol and restaurant groups in this case) want legislative action that benefits their bottom line, they contribute substantial amounts of money, and they get what they want.

But the money = votes equation is complicated by the fact that in October 2000, Congress *passed* the lower drunk driving standard as part of the 2001 Department of Transportation appropriations bill. Under the law, which Clinton signed on October 23, 2000, states that do not adopt a .08 percent blood alcohol level for drunk driving by 2004 will lose their federal highway funds.[15] After fighting tighter drunk driving standards for a decade, and after winning time after time, the alcohol industry and restaurants lost.

While the outcome of this case—demonstrably not in the industry's interest—suggests that money does not always buy votes, an examination of the congressional vote casts even more doubt about what money does. According to the CRP's data, key interest groups (beer, wine, and liquor producers and wholesalers, and restaurant and bar groups) contributed over $7 million to House members between 1997 and 2000. The groups added another $8 million in soft money over the same period. What did they get for their money?

Not much. The transportation bill passed overwhelmingly, 344–50 in the House. Although the legislation addressed many issues besides the blood alcohol level provision, it is apparent that alcohol or restaurant money played no role in the vote: the 344 House members who voted "yes" received, on average, $16,931 between 1997 and 2000; those who voted "no," in the industry's favor, received $16,171. The industry actually gave more to its opponents than it did to its supporters. Moreover, there is no relationship between large contributions and the vote: of the 394 House members who voted, 207 received at least

---

[13]Common Cause, *Paying the Price: How Tobacco, Gun, Gambling, & Alcohol Interests Block Common Sense Solutions to Some of the Nation's Most Urgent Problems,* June 2000, 15.

[14]Center for Responsive Politics, "Happy Hour: The Alcohol Industry, Restaurants & Drunk Driving." Money in Politics Alert, 5:49 (June 19, 2000) (http://www. opensecrets.org/alerts/v5/alertv5_49.htm).

[15]Steven A. Holmes, "House and Senate Agree on Drunken-Driving Law," *New York Times,* October 4, 2000.

$10,000 in industry campaign contributions. Eighty-seven percent voted "yes." 187 House members received less than $10,000. Exactly the same percentage voted "yes."

Plumbing the depths of the legislative process further yields no more evidence of money buying votes. The .08 percent provision was added to the transportation bill in conference. Members of the House conference committee—who agreed to attach the .08 percent provision to the transportation bill—received an average of $14,090 from the industry, or less than the average opponent of the provision.

In this case, legislators directly contradicted the expectations of the standard campaign finance reform template. On the federal drunk driving standard, powerful interests put their money into Congress, members looked at which side gave them the most, and then did exactly the reverse of what they should have done if money were the deciding factor.

Conclusion

What do these four cases suggest? Certainly not that campaign money plays no role in congressional outcomes. Indeed, drawing that conclusion would be just as incorrect as using four contrary examples to prove that money always determines the outcome. Instead, the main lesson is that legislative outcomes are complex and are almost always oversimplified by one-dimensional accounts connecting campaign contributions directly to congressional decisions.

Oversimplification does several things, none of which is helpful to the debate over campaign finance reform. First, as I noted above, it creates the impression that *everyone* is hopelessly corrupt and that money is the determining factor in key governmental decisions (when, in fact, this conclusion is in many cases demonstrably untrue). By repeatedly falling back on simplistic explanations that in many cases fail to meet the basic logical standards of social science argument, those who advocate reform make it much harder to distinguish true corruption from the inevitable compromises and deals that are part of any nontrivial legislation.

Second, oversimplification creates an unrealistic impression that political decisions should, somehow, be hermetically sealed off from those who want to have a say in those decisions and that there is an objective "truth" that is corrupted and distorted by lobbying and campaign contributions. The difficulty with this notion, as historian Alan Brinkley has persuasively argued, is that it is simply false:

> The belief that a pure "public interest" exists somewhere as a kernel of true knowledge untainted by politics or parochialism, and that it provides not just an array of basic principles but a concrete set of solutions to complex problems, is

an attractive notion, but it is also a myth. We may be able to agree on a broad framework of beliefs capable of organizing our political life, but any such framework will have to make room within it for conflicting concepts of how to translate those beliefs into practice.[16]

The result of these two fallacies—magnified by the tendency of reformers to substitute advocacy for analysis—probably makes effective reform less likely, because if voters see the problem as *politics,* and not money, then it makes no difference whether private money is driven out of campaigns or not. Either way, we're left with venal politicians and a corrupt process, so why bother? Post-reform, the system will be just as bad as it was before (surely this is one reason why public financing for legislative elections is usually viewed as welfare for politicians). The rhetorical strategies almost certainly contribute to the disconnect between the public's belief that the campaign finance system is fundamentally flawed and the lack of any real pressure for reform. Oversimplification encourages individuals to reach firm conclusions about what is wrong with the campaign finance system, even when they have no, or provably incorrect, information.[17]

Ultimately, too much of the campaign finance reform literature refuses to accept the notion that politics is mostly about self interest—a reality readily acknowledged by the Founding Fathers, although even they expressed disappointment at how quickly it came to dominate decision making—and that the purpose of governing institutions is to find ways of melding competing interests into a consensus that approximates whatever we decide to define as the "public interest." Meaningful and effective reform is not possible without such recognition. And forcing complex legislative processes into a simplistic "money = votes" mold is not the way to get there.

---

[16]Alan Brinkley, "The Challenge to Deliberative Democracy," in *The New Federalist Papers,* Alan Brinkley, Nelson W. Polsby, and Kathleen M. Sullivan, eds. (New York: W. W. Norton & Co., 1997), 26.

[17]In a late-April 2001 poll, only one respondent in five knew that the Senate had approved the McCain-Feingold campaign finance reform bill (almost three weeks after the bill had passed). Fifteen percent incorrectly said that the Senate had voted down the bill, and 64 percent said they did not know one way or the other. In contrast, 46 percent knew that the Senate had scaled back Bush's tax cut proposal; 57 percent knew that Bush had proposed an increase in federal education spending; and 28 percent knew that Bush had decided not to place limits on power plant carbon dioxide emissions (http://www. people-press.org/april01que.htm).

Chapter 5

Sources and Uses of Soft Money:
What Do We Know?

Ray La Raja

Reading the editorial pages of our nation's newspapers one would think that the only solution to campaign finance problems is to eliminate soft money, the funds that parties raise without caps. It is no surprise, then, that the centerpiece of reform legislation winding its way through Congress is a ban on soft money. But we really know relatively little about how political parties raise and spend soft money. Data on soft money has only been available in the past few election cycles, and there have been just a handful of scholarly studies of party activity with soft money.

One reason we know so little is that the advocates of reform have cast the debate narrowly on the problem of corruption. Since soft money contributions have no limits the potential for corruption would also appear to be boundless. So, attacking what they perceive as the most pernicious problem in the system, reformers target soft money, and their primary objective is to prevent the *quid pro quo* between contributor and politician. Because the corruption perspective dominates the debate—even though scholars lack hard evidence to demonstrate corruption—other concerns about campaign finance receive scant attention. (See Ken Mayer's chapter for a lively critique of the corruption perspective.)

In practice, any system of campaign finance touches on a number of important political values in addition to the desire for clean elections. These values reflect widely accepted concerns about democratic participation, fairness, and accountability. For instance, Wilcox, in his chapter, introduces the point that contributions to campaigns are a form of political participation, and campaign finance regimes should be designed to encourage greater participation. To promote fairness and accountability, Americans would surely value a campaign finance system that gives challengers a decent opportunity to compete, and perhaps even to win elections. It is important to ask whether removing resources from the system advances or hinders competition. From the perspective of many political scientists, a campaign finance regime should support healthy parties because these organizations provide important cues to voters and help manage conflicts among diverse interests.

In short, a robust debate on campaign finance should consider a range of political values before coming to judgment about the merits of proposed reforms. But if reformers want to talk knowledgeably about the pros and cons of various policies, we need good information about how the system currently works. As far as soft money goes, our collective knowledge is minimal, even though the nation's lawmakers are on the threshold of passing reforms that would eliminate this source of party funds. To paraphrase Winston Churchill on the RAF, rarely have so many sought such far-reaching reform on the basis of so little knowledge.

This chapter explores the contours of party soft money to see what we might be gaining and losing by such a ban. Soft money is supposed to be used for party building and not direct candidate support. Party-building activities support headquarter operations (salaries, rent, office equipment), voter registration, mobilization, and traditional party "hoopla" such as passing out campaign banners, yard signs, and bumper stickers. Parties do use some soft money to help federal candidates, a practice that violates the spirit, if not the letter of the law. And, to the extent that parties use money to support federal candidates they challenge federal campaign finance laws that limit contributions to candidates, particularly the laws prohibiting contributions from corporations and unions.

My analysis first observes the *sources* of soft money, evaluating which groups contribute to the two major parties and who appears to benefit from such contributions. I then go on to look at the *uses* of soft money, assessing the parties' commitment to genuine party building versus so-called "issue ads" that tend to support specific candidates in violation of federal law. What follows is a preliminary step toward laying empirical foundations for an improved understanding of the sources and uses of party money.

Business interests are by far the dominant contributors of soft money, but their share of total donations has not risen in the last three election cycles ending in 1998. Other groups, such as labor, provide significant in-kind benefits to parties, in addition to cash donations, that make the business advantage appear less impressive. Republicans, who receive most of these business contributions, appear to benefit more than Democrats from a campaign finance system that permits soft money contributions in unlimited amounts. On the other hand, Democrats appear to use soft money in ways that make up for their deficiency of hard money relative to the Republicans.

The section on uses of soft money demonstrates a far more complex reality about how parties spend soft money than conventional accounts suggest. While parties use a lot of soft money to pay for "issue ads" that support presidential or congressional candidates, they also continue to spend a great deal of soft money on traditional party-building functions that mobilize voters through individual contacts. While expenditures on media-related activities surged in 1996, so did spending on grassroots and voter mobilization efforts—exactly the kind of party campaign activity Congress wanted to encourage when it revised the FECA in 1979.

These findings, especially regarding soft money spending, complicate the reform debate considerably. On one hand, parties appear to violate the spirit, if not the letter, of the law when they pay for issue ads with soft money. But they also use soft money to bolster party activities that citizens, elected officials and political scientists view as positive for democracy. The parties are spending more soft money on political rallies, bumper stickers and yard signs, and voter identification and get-out-the-vote programs, as well as augmented activities at party headquarters. In short, it appears that party organizations are stronger and increasingly active in campaigns.

Sources of Soft Money

Soft Money Total Receipts Are Rising

Since the FEC began requiring parties to report soft money contributions in 1992, receipts have clearly escalated. The amount of soft money raised by both parties tripled between 1992 and 1996 (from $85.9 to $261.9 million). In the 2000 elections, it more than doubled to $467.5 from 1996 (see Table 5.1). It also doubled between the midterm years, from $101.6 million in 1994 to $224.4 million in 1998. Although the FEC does not provide data for earlier years, campaign finance scholars estimate that the rate of growth for soft money during the 1980s was significantly lower.[1]

The value of soft money increased in the 1996 elections because political entrepreneurs in both parties figured out how to use it to air political advertisements that benefited federal candidates. Party-sponsored ads promoted the presi-

---

[1] Herbert E. Alexander, "Financing the 1976 Election," (Washington, D.C.: Congressional Quarterly, 1979), p. 190; Anthony Corrado, *Paying for Presidents* (New York: Twentieth Century Fund, 1993), p. 67.

Table 5.1. Contributions in Parties, 1992–2000 (in millions of dollars)

	Federal (hard money)	Nonfederal (soft money)	percent soft money
1992			
Democrats	89.6	36.2	29%
Republicans	192.1	49.7	21%
1994			
Democrats	77.2	49.1	39%
Republicans	169.1	52.5	24%
1996			
Democrats	128.4	123.8	49%
Republicans	288.0	138.1	32%
1998			
Democrats	96.6	92.8	49%
Republicans	195.6	131.6	40%
2000			
Democrats	206.8	243.1	54%
Republicans	345.0	224.4	39%

Source: *Federal Elections Commission*
Note: *Amounts reflect national party figures only.*

dential campaigns of Bill Clinton and Bob Dole but avoided explicit electioneering messages that would have compelled the parties to use hard money. Their success in the presidential arena encouraged the parties to use issue ads in House and Senate campaigns.

The pressure to find loopholes in the campaign finance laws had been building for some time. As campaigns became more expensive in the 1990s, due to increasing technology costs and an intense battle for control of Congress, parties sought new ways to support candidates whose fundraising was restricted by FECA limits on individual contributions to $1,000 and PAC contributions to $5,000 per election. The limits, which are not indexed to inflation, have not keep pace with rising campaign costs,[2] and the pressure to find new sources of income led party leaders to seek a less restricted source of campaign funds—soft money.

A 1979 amendment to FECA permitted parties to use soft money for "party-building" activities such as voter identification and mobilization. The parties used this amendment to expand the boundaries of "party building" so they could help candidates more directly. By law, parties are only allowed to contribute $5,000 to House candidates and $17,500 to Senate candidates, and to provide limited in-kind support called coordinated expenditures. But parties found ways to target soft money for mobilization activities and issue ads in important federal contests. By claiming to pursue party building, they could raise and spend soft money and channel it into competitive races.

The parties appear to be relying more and more on soft money to fund their activities. The proportion of total party receipts coming from soft money increased substantially during the past two election cycles. Democrats, the relatively poorer party with hard money, rely more on soft money than Republicans. In 1992, soft money constituted 29 percent of Democratic receipts and 21 percent of Republican receipts at the national level (see Table 5.1). In the last two presidential election cycles, about half of Democratic receipts came from soft money, while Republican soft money accounted for about 40 percent of their budget.[3] If soft money were banned, the parties would lose a significant source of their funding.

Who Contributes?

Business interests have been the leading soft money contributors since the Federal Elections Commission (FEC) instituted disclosure requirements in 1992. In 1993–94, business interests gave a total of $56 million to both parties. This

---

[2]According to Committee for the Study of the American Electorate, these cost increases are apparently due to the increased reliance of political campaigns on expensive forms of media, such as television, rather than inflation for media costs per se. See the report, "Use of Media Principal Reason Campaign Costs Skyrocket" (Washington, D.C.: Committee for the Study of the American Electorate, 1996).

[3]This analysis includes the national committees only. For the Democrats, these include the Democratic National Committee, the Democratic Senatorial Campaign Committee and the Democratic Congressional Campaign Committee. For the Republicans, these include the Republican National Committee, the National Republican Senate Committee and the National Republican Congressional Committee.

figure more than doubled to $122.8 million in 1997–98 (see Table 5.2). Individuals, the next largest group of donors, contributed $20.4 million in 1993–94, and doubled this in 1997–98, giving $52.4 million. Labor contributions during this same period doubled from $4.8 million to $10.3 million. There are other groups that give soft money, i.e., political clubs, ideological groups, candidate committees, although their contributions to the parties are small compared to business and individual contributions.

While donations from all these sources have increased dramatically in terms of absolute dollars, the percentage of money from each source has remained fairly constant over the past three election cycles. From 1993–1998, for example, business donations constituted approximately 63 percent of total soft money donations. Individuals contributed approximately 25 percent of the total, and labor money comprised about 5 percent per election cycle.[4] It is worth exploring whether the supply of political money in a given donor pool reached its outer limit in the 2000 elections when soft money receipts doubled. A number of businesses, for instance, decided to forego soft money contributions because senior executives wanted to distance themselves from the appearance of participating in corrupt exchanges or felt they were not getting enough in return for the contributions.[5]

The fact that business interests dominate soft money contributions renews a dilemma confronted by the Progressive movement at the turn of the century. At that time reformers pressed for legislation to curb the growing political power of emerging corporate wealth. Congress responded in 1907 by outlawing contributions to presidential and congressional candidates by corporations and banks. But this effort and subsequent legislation during the century failed to stem the flow of corporate money into politics until the passage of the FECA in 1974, which prohibited the establishment of "volunteer" committees to funnel money to candidates, and limited individual contributions to $1,000 per candidate per election. These constraints on outside committee and individual contributions encouraged the proliferation of Political Action Committees (PACs) to raise funds from members of the same organization for political contributions. The PAC system appeared to prevent "fat cats" from giving large, under-the-table contributions since PACs are permitted to contribute just $5,000 per candidate per election and are required to disclose the sources and uses of their funds. Party soft money, which lacks contribution limits and full disclosure requirements, seems to undermine the goal of preventing corporations and other cash-rich institutions or individuals from using their wealth to influence politics.

---

[4]Fundraising in the 2000 election cycle clearly outpaced earlier cycles. As of this writing, I have not analyzed the 2000 election finances so it remains to be seen whether any of these groups will fall behind because they have been "tapped out."

[5]Don Van Natta, Jr. "As Political Gifts Set a Record Pace, Some Quit Giving," *The New York Times*, May 2, 2000, p. A1.

Table 5.2. Contributions by Group, 1994–1998 (in millions of dollars)

	1994	% of total	1996	% of total	1998	% of total
Business	56.0	64%	149.3	62%	122.8	64%
Individuals	20.4	23%	69.1	29%	52.4	27%
Labor Organizations	4.8	6%	9.6	4%	10.3	5%
Political Parties and Clubs	3.0	3%	8.7	4%	1.8	1%
Political Candidate Committees	0.5	1%	0.6	0%	0.9	0%
Other Organizations	3.0	3%	2.9	1%	2.4	1%
Total Contributions	87.8	100%	240.2	100%	190.7	100%

Source: FECInfo at http://www.tray.com/fecinfo/
Note: Figures do not match FEC totals in Table 1 exactly because the above does not include nonitemized (<$200) contributions.

Defenders of corporate contributions argue that business organizations often compete against one another to gain policies favorable to their specific organizational interests. In other words, businesses do not uniformly prefer one set of policies. If Madison's theory in *Federalist 10* concerning factions anticipates the reality of contribution patterns, then the influence of soft money could be a wash when the interests of many and varied donors are taken into account. In other words, when parties receive donations from competing interests, they will not be unduly influenced by any set of donors. Still, one would want to feel assured that the interests of a broader collective—consumers, for instance—are considered with comparable weight even though they lack organizations contributing soft money to the parties.

The dominance of business over labor money should be considered in light of labor's heavy involvement in political campaigns through in-kind services to candidates. While labor only gives less than 10 percent of the soft money that business interests provide, labor organizations provide considerable resources to parties in the form of voter mobilization programs that overwhelmingly support Democrats. There are no reliable estimates of how much labor spends in campaigns on their own since they do not have to report all their activities to the FEC. We know, however, that the AFL-CIO spent $35 million in 1996 on campaign activities in key congressional districts, including an estimated $22 million on issue ads.[6] When we add these in-kind sums to the cash that labor organizations contribute to parties, business dominance appears less striking.

Ideological groups donate surprisingly little soft money to parties. But they, like labor organizations, are well placed to contact and mobilize members on their own rather than provide cash to the parties. In fact, some of these organizations have more to gain from running campaigns independently because they can tailor messages to suit their particular agenda.[7] For instance, a pro-environmental or antitax organization might attempt to shape a presidential campaign around issues that are meaningful to members by placing issue ads in important media markets.[8]

---

[6]See Committee for Economic Development, *Investing in the People's Business: A Business Proposal for Campaign Finance Reform* (New York: Committee for Economic Development), 29.

[7]For more on outside spending in federal campaigns see David Magleby, ed., *Outside Money: Soft Money and Issue Advocacy in the 1998 Congressional Elections* (New York: Rowman and Littlefield, 2000).

[8]Jim VandeHei, "Gun-control Efforts Trigger Strong NRA Drive for GOP," *The Wall Street Journal,* May 5, 2000, A18. Until recently, many of these organizations were not required to report the sources and uses of campaign money. On July 1, 2000, President Clinton signed into law a bill that obligates groups organized under Section 527 of the tax code to disclose their political activities. Under Public Law 106–230, Section 527 groups are required to notify the IRS of their existence within 24 hours of organizing and to file periodic reports disclosing their contributions and expenditures.

Election-related spending since 1994 indicates that campaign activity by noncandidate committees increasingly may impact election outcomes.[9] Given this trend and the current legal environment framed by *Buckley v. Valeo,* there is reason to believe that ideological organizations and other nonparty or noncandidate organizations will gain more influence if soft money is banned. Lacking soft money, parties may use surrogates to perform many of the campaign activities they now perform themselves. One problem with this arrangement is that voters will not be able to link campaign messages to party candidates since the surrogate organizations often assume unfamiliar or uninformative names. The benefit of partisan labels that provide voters with useful information about candidates will likely diminish the more that outside groups engage independently in federal campaigns.

Partisan Advantages?

Another concern raised at the outset is the issue of equity between the two major parties. Does the current campaign finance system, which permits soft money, favor one party over the other? Maintaining a competitive party system requires attention to the electoral regulatory structures that allocate benefits among participants. If soft money provides significant leverage to one party we should be concerned whether this imbalance distorts the legitimate representation of varied interests in the nation. Understanding who benefits the most from soft money also provides insights into prospects for reform. For meaningful reform to proceed, contending parties must reach compromises that account for the consequences of policy proposals. Neither Republican nor Democratic leaders will want to change the status quo, so long as there is considerable uncertainty about how reform proposals will alter the competitive advantage of either party.

My findings suggest that Democrats might accrue short-term benefits from gathering soft money since it potentially frees up hard money resources that they lack in comparison to Republicans. On the other hand, long-term trends do not augur well for Democrats since the Republicans may be able to seize control of both Congress and the White House; and they have ties to business groups that provide the bulk of soft money.

The Republicans increased their soft money lead over the Democrats during the 1997–98 election cycle but the Democrats regained equal footing in 2000 (Table 5.1). But the Democrats relied on President Clinton, a prolific fundraiser, to attract contributions during the past eight years. It remains to be seen whether the Democrats can continue to draw contributions as well as the Republicans in

---

[9]Magleby, 2000.

the 2002 elections, especially since President Bush demonstrated formidable fundraising ability in the 2000 elections.

Table 5.3 demonstrates considerable differences between the parties with respect to the donor groups that provide soft money. Business organizations contribute more to Republicans, while organized labor favors Democrats almost exclusively. Corporations do not use soft money more heavily than hard money to support Republicans. In the 1997–98 election, corporations contributed 68 percent of their soft money to the Republican party, the same percentage that corporate PACs gave in hard money to Republican congressional candidates.[10] The soft money regime, so far, does not apparently skew business contributions even more in favor of Republicans, a good sign for the Democrats.

Another critical reason the Republicans dominate soft money receipts is that they are the majority party in Congress. Since the Republicans gained control of Congress in 1994, soft money donors are increasingly likely to support them over Democrats. This pattern is consistent with past studies that demonstrate interest group support favors incumbents and the party that controls the government.[11] Democratic party's control of the presidency, while beneficial for fundraising, was not sufficient to alter the business contributions in favor of them. For interest groups seeking particular benefits it is probably more strategic to create good will with individual members of Congress who oversee the details of legislation than with the president.

As expected, a Democratic advantage exists among labor organizations. In 1998, labor interests donated $10.3 million to the Democrats and only $390,000 to Republicans. While labor's contributions to Democrats pale in comparison to business' $122 million, labor provides considerable in-kind support to Democratic candidates. Local labor councils mobilize union members through canvassing, phone banks, and newsletters, while national and state organizations support favored candidates through issue ads. Republicans argue, with good reason, that labor activities constitute a considerable chunk of in-kind benefits to Democratic candidates. Indeed, banning soft money would do little to diminish the benefits that Democrats derive from labor campaign activity.[12] For all practical purposes,

---

[10]Federal contribution data from the Federal Election Commission, "FEC Releases Information on PAC Activity for 1997–98" Press Release, June 8, 1999 at http://www.fec.gov/press/paccin98.htm. Soft Money contribution data from FECinfo, "Soft Money Summary," December 28, 1998 at http://www.tray.com/cgi-win/_smrpt.exe.

[11]See for example, Frank J. Sorauf, *Inside Campaign Finance* (New Haven: Yale University, 1992) and Gary C. Jacobson, *Money in Congressional Elections* (New Haven: Yale University, 1980).

[12]One way to limit labor unions from helping Democratic candidates is to prohibit labor unions from airing issue ads in the weeks prior to an election. This proposal is part of a McCain-Feingold campaign finance reform bill (S.27) now being considered in the 107th Congress.

Table 5.3. Partisan Differences Among Contributors, 1994, 1996, and 1998 elections

	1993–94	1995–96	1997–98
Business			
Democrats	$23,673,849	$62,379,704	$39,639,974
Republicans	$32,353,685	$86,436,151	$83,071,405
% to Republicans	58%	58%	68%
Labor			
Democrats	$4,767,595	$9,358,589	$9,949,093
Republicans	$64,530	$239,985	$390,500
% to Republicans	1%	3%	4%
Individuals			
Democrats	$10,091,251	$36,201,377	$26,072,402
Republicans	$10,275,323	$32,233,875	$25,983,634
% to Republicans	50%	47%	50%

Source: *FECinfo at http://www.tray.com/fecinfo/*

labor activities are funded by soft money except that labor organizations rather than the parties control how it is spent. Thus, Republicans argue, party-controlled soft money helps even the playing field for Republican candidates.

The parties have achieved parity with respect to the amount of soft money from individual donors. In 1993–94 they both received about $10 million from individual contributors, and they raised $26 million from individuals in the 1997–1998 mid-term elections. During the presidential election in 1996, Democrats pulled in $36 million, just $4 million more than Republicans. The Democrats rely on larger contributions among fewer donors to achieve these equal outcomes. The average soft money contribution to Democratic party committees in the 1998 election cycle was about $17,300, while the average contribution to Republicans was a little over $7,000.[13]

Democrats could be hurt by reforms that permit soft money in relatively small contributions, say, under the Democratic average of $17,300. The Repub-

---

[13]These figures reflect total contributions by a donor to the House, Senate or National party committees.

lican contributor base is at least four times larger than the Democrat's for contributions less than $10,000.[14] Democrats might prefer a ban on soft money rather than continuing a soft money regime with low limits, since Republicans have a larger base of small and moderate contributors. But raising hard money contribution limits could hurt Democrats if soft money is banned.

The relatively low figures for average contributions provide a striking contrast to the huge sums reported frequently in the news media. Certainly, to the extent that parties rely on super donors for their resources, we should be concerned about parties and party leaders being beholden to them. An analysis conducted by the Center for Responsive Politics revealed that donors who gave more than $120,000 (only about 800 individuals and organizations) accounted for close to $300 million in soft money, or 60 percent of the funds parties received. These figures suggest the parties rely excessively on super donors who are less two percent of soft money contributors. An obvious remedy is to limit the size of soft money contributions to a level that does not seem corrupting. But reformers who focus exclusively on the potential problems caused by super donors obscure the fact that there exists a significant pool of resources available to parties in increments below $25,000. In 1998, for instance, 93 percent of soft money donors gave less than $25,000, which comprised almost a quarter of party soft money. By banning soft money, parties would lose access to resources that almost certainly do not have the potentially corrupting effect of the $100,000+ donations.

Spending Soft Money

To understand how parties use soft money, I observed the federal reports submitted to the FEC by the 100 state parties for election cycles 1992 through 1998.[15] Much activity with soft money takes place at the state level because campaign finance rules provide incentives to use soft money for state and local party building. State parties raise substantial amounts of soft money and receive transfers of soft money from national committees.

---

[14]The number of donors who gave less than $10,000 is 3,116 for Democrats and 12,650 for Republicans. This does not include the numerous non-itemized contributors who gave less than $200.

[15]Using files compiles by the FEC, I developed a coding scheme to categorize more than 300,000 itemized expenditure entries in each election cycle. See Table 5 for categories.

Are State Parties Spending More Soft Money?

State parties are more active than ever in election campaigns. Combined soft and hard money spending in state party federal accounts almost doubled between 1992 and 1996. Undoubtedly, some of this spending is the product of "pass throughs," transfers from the national to state parties to purchase issue ads and other services in support of federal candidates. But state parties have also increased spending on campaign activities that serve party building functions.

The use of soft money has spurred much of this growth. In the 1996 presidential election the 100 state parties spent $178 million, almost triple the amount of soft money spent in 1992. Between the 1994 and 1998 midterm elections the parties doubled their use of soft money, spending a record $187 million. Hard money expenditures have also risen but not at the same rate. Since FEC rules require soft-hard matching for each campaign activity, hard money spending increases with soft money spending. It appears, however, that soft money pays for a larger portion of activities with each passing election cycle. In 1998, for the first time since 1992 when state parties were required to report soft money finances, they spent more soft than hard money in their federal accounts (see Figure 5.1).

The shift from hard to soft money is not difficult to explain. Soft money is easier to obtain since there are no limits on contributions to parties, except when states regulate party fundraising. A party that wants to preserve hard money for candidate contributions and coordinated expenditures in federal elections will purchase goods and services with soft money whenever possible. Over the four most recent election cycles, the state parties have learned how to match soft and hard money expenditures to maximize the use of the former. One indication that parties behave this way is that direct state party support for federal candidates, mostly in the form of coordinated expenditures increased from $5 million in 1996 to $18 million in 1998.[16] Most likely, state parties substituted soft for hard money when paying for many campaign activities, thereby freeing up hard money for direct candidate support.[17]

An important question is whether soft money reported in the federal accounts of state parties is actually controlled by the national parties, whose primary interest is to elect candidates for federal office. To the extent that the national party supports the state parties through transfers, one can infer that they have some control over state party expenditures. Table 5.4 gives a sense of how

---

[16]Source: Federal Elections Commission at FEC http://www.fec.gov/press/ptyye98.htm.

[17]This substitution effect is attenuated probably because most state parties relinquish their authority to contribute to federal candidates to the national committees through agency agreements. See Dwyre (1996) for a more thorough examination of this process.

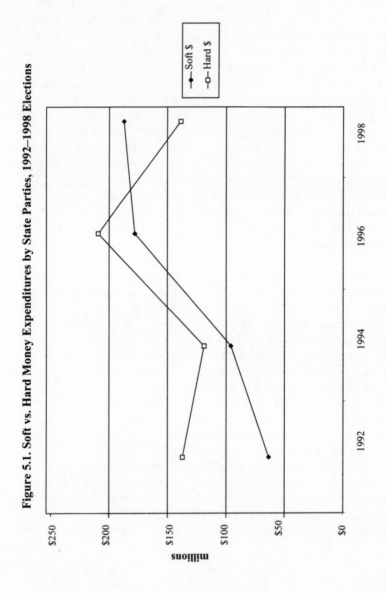

Figure 5.1. Soft vs. Hard Money Expenditures by State Parties, 1992–1998 Elections

much state parties rely financially on the national parties. The national parties supported a larger percentage of state party budgets in 1996 and 1998 than they did earlier, suggesting that they have more influence in state party affairs than in earlier elections. Prior to 1996, national party transfers accounted for less than 14 percent of the federal accounts of state committees. In the 1996 and 1998 elections, this portion grew to 42 percent and 31 percent respectively. Table 5.4 also illustrates that state parties rely more heavily on national parties for soft money than hard money. National parties provide just under a quarter of the hard money state parties spend, but 65 percent of the soft money they spent in 1996 and 37 percent in 1998. It appears that soft money has become a primary means of intra-party support. State parties continue to raise the majority of funds on their own—indeed, they raise more money independently than ever before—but they receive significant support from the national parties. In addition to party transfers, some journalistic accounts report that state parties benefit from soft money contributors who are encouraged to donate to state parties by officials of the national party.[18]

Since national parties provide as much as one-third of state party funds, it is reasonable to assume that portions of soft money from the national parties are targeted to achieve national party goals, which may differ from the priorities of state organizations. These data demonstrate unequivocally that the direction of resource flows between parties has reversed since the 1960s, when national parties had to solicit contributions from state affiliates. Heard (1960) predicted such a change would create opportunities for party integration and growth, even as it augmented tensions among party levels.[19]

To summarize, soft money spending by state parties has risen each year since 1992, and outpaced hard money spending in 1998. FEC matching requirements ensure that soft money spending will not eclipse hard money spending, but it appears parties exploit allocation rules to spend soft rather than hard money. State parties raise and spend increasing sums of hard money, funds that meet all the requirements of the FECA. Hard money spending doubled between the 1992 and 1996 elections and the state parties raise three-fourths of this money themselves. The prospect of securing soft money from the national parties may spur state parties to engage more effectively in raising hard money, precisely because of the federal matching requirements. I also find evidence that soft money spent on administrative chores frees hard money for contributions and coordinated expenditures in support of federal candidates.

---

[18]Ira Chinoy and Dan Morgan, "DNC Channeled Donations to State Parties, *Washington Post,* January 26, 1997.

[19]Alexander Heard, *The Costs of Democracy* (Chapel Hill: University of North Carolina, 1960).

Table 5.4. State Party Spending and National Party Support, 1992–1998 Elections (in thousands of dollars)

	1992	1994	1996	1998
Soft Money				
State Party Expenditures	$63	$96	$178	$187
National Party Transfers	$18	$18	$115	$69
Percent provided by National Party	29%	19%	65%	37%
Hard Money				
State Party Expenditures	$137	$119	$209	$139
National Party Transfers	$10	$10	$48	$32
Percent provided by National Party	7%	8%	23%	23%
TOTALS				
State Party Expenditures	$201	$215	$387	$325
National Party Transfers	$28	$28	$162	$101
Percent provided by National Party	14%	13%	42%	31%

Source: *Federal Elections Commission*

How Do State Political Parties Spend Soft Money?

There is anecdotal evidence, mostly from the news media, describing the use of soft money for issue ads. More systematic scholarly research demonstrates that in key races soft money is invested in the ground war of campaigns—contacts with individual voters using direct mail and telephone banks.[20] Party and campaign finance scholars continue to speculate whether the infusion of soft money in the last two decades has altered patterns of state party activity. Advocates of stronger parties argue that providing parties with privileged access to campaign resources would reverse the long decline of party organizations. From their perspective, the introduction of soft money into the party system provides an interesting test case for this theory. How will parties behave with this new wealth generated by soft money? Will they spend additional increments to build the party through voter identification programs and grassroots activity?

---

[20]David Magleby, 2000.

Or will soft money simply buttress candidate-centered campaigns, with the parties serving as pass-throughs to pay for television ads promoting individual nominees?

My findings will satisfy neither side in the debate over whether soft money is good or bad for the party system. I find elements of what some would consider "bad" as well as "good" spending. On the positive side, state organizations continue to use funds in ways traditionally expected of parties: to mobilize voters, to disseminate grassroots paraphernalia like bumper stickers, and to maintain the organization through payments of rent and salaries. In short, soft money enables parties to spend additional resources on party-building activities.

The 1996 election, however, marked a dramatic shift toward greater spending on media related activities. Whereas state parties spent just three percent of their budgets on media activities in the 1992 presidential election, four years later this category absorbed more than one-third of their budgets. The shift is even more striking in absolute terms: media spending jumped from about $2 million to $65 million (see Table 5.5). The reasons for this shift have been explained in many journalistic accounts of the 1996 and 1998 campaigns.[21] The increase in media spending in 1996 was a result of campaign strategies pursued by the parties and presidential candidates to saturate critical electoral markets with televised issue ads that benefited the candidates in all but name. Dick Morris, the key Clinton-Gore campaign strategist, urged the DNC to begin televising issue ads in the summer and early fall as a way to shore up a faltering Clinton early in the election and undercut the presumptive GOP nominee, Bob Dole. The RNC, in support of the Dole-Kemp ticket, countered with the same strategy right before and after the convention in July. Apparently, both national parties tried to take advantage of the favorable soft-hard ratios available to state parties by making them responsible for purchasing ads.

Ironically, soft money spending on issue ads might be an artifact of the sweeping reforms of 1974 that established a system of public financing for presidential candidates. If a candidate accepts public funding in the primary he faces limits on spending in each state. A competitive race could cause candidates to bump up against these limits rather early in the primary season, especially given the trend toward front-loading of primaries, forcing the candidate to curtail spending severely during the weeks leading up to the convention. Bob Dole faced several tough and well-funded challengers in 1996. He was forced to spend money fending off Gramm, Buchanan, and Forbes.[22] At the same time, Clinton was using party soft money, as well as primary campaign funds, to at-

---

[21]See, for example, Elizabeth Drew, *Whatever It Takes* (New York: Viking, 1997).

[22]Wesley Joe and Clyde Wilcox, "Financing the 1996 Presidential Nominations: The Last Regulated Campaign?" in *Financing the 1996 Election,* ed. John Green (Armonk, N.Y.: Sharpe, 1999), 37–62.

Table 5.5. State Party Soft Money Expenditures by Category, 1992–1998 elections (in millions of dollars)

	1992	%	1994	%	1996	%	1998	%
Administrative/Overhead	42.3	67%	62.7	65%	72.2	41%	107.3	57%
Media	1.9	3%	3.5	4%	64.7	36%	30.2	16%
Mobilization	8.6	14%	14.9	16%	16.0	9%	22.6	12%
Traditional Party Hoopla	1.2	2%	3.3	3%	8.3	5%	6.4	3%
Multicandidate contributions	1.5	2%	1.5	2%	0.4	0%	2.1	1%
Fundraising	4.7	7%	4.8	5%	8.6	5%	10.0	5%
Unidentified	3.3	5%	5.1	5%	7.4	4%	8.3	4%
TOTAL	63.4	100%	96.0	100%	177.7	100%	186.8	100%
N	100		100		100		100	

Source: Federal Elections Commission

Code: Administrative/Overhead = office-related expenses such as rent, salaries, computers, travel, and utilities

Media = communication expenditures for television, radio, and newspaper, and production and purchase costs.

Mobilization = costs of contacting individual voters through direct mail, telephone banks, canvassing, and voter identification files.

Traditional Party Hoopla = yard signs, bumper stickers, banners, pins, palm cards, rallies, fairs.

Multicandidate contributions = nongeneric in-kind contributions from the party to several candidates, e.g., newspaper ads, that jointly benefit specific federal and state candidates.

Fundraising = costs associated with joint fundraising for federal, state, and local campaigns.

Unidentified = expenditures that could not be determined from FEC reports.

tack the GOP and promote his campaign themes for the general election. Dole and the Republicans could only retaliate with party soft money ads, given that the candidate would not receive additional public funds for the general election until after the convention. The late timing of FEC-released public funds leaves a good part of the summer in which either candidate can harm the other through attack ads. The parties got into the campaign, in part, to bridge the period between when a nominee effectively, but not officially, wins the nomination, and the official start of the general election season.

The increasing use of soft money for issue ads may also reflect the inadequacy of a public funding system for presidential campaigns that fails to keep pace with rising media costs. An inflation adjuster covers some of the rise in media costs, but fails to address a substantive change in campaigns during the last two decades. A study by the Committee for the Study of the American Electorate (1996) shows that campaign strategists rely increasingly on expensive media-related activities, especially television, that drive up the cost of the campaign.[23]

During midterm elections, spending on media decreases without the demands of a national campaign. In the 1998 midterm, the amount spent on media-related activities by state parties was cut more than half, to $30 million from two years earlier. But this amount was 10 times as much as party spending on similar activities in the 1994 midterm election. The lessons of using party soft money for issue ads in the 1996 presidential campaign had obviously been passed on for congressional elections. According to a study sponsored by the Brennan Center, party spending on issue ads—which includes both state and national organizations—amounted to $25.9 million.[24] This spending accounted for close to 45,000 ads, reflecting about 20 percent of all campaign advertising.

The data demonstrate clearly that soft money was transferred to state parties to fund media-related activity that comprised mostly issue ads.[25] Yet not all national party transfers were spent on issue ads. At most, state parties spent 55 percent of transfers on issue ads in 1996, and 43 percent on them in 1998.[26] Where did the rest of the soft money go? The answer is that parties used "ex-

---

[23]See Committee for the Study of the American Electorate, 1996.

[24]Krasno, Jonathan and Daniel E. Seltz, Buying Time: Television Advertising in the 1998 Congressional Elections (New York: Brennan Center for Justice at NYU School of Law, 2000).

[25]The Krasno and Seltz figures that include party spending at all levels suggest that my data may overestimate the amount spent by state parties on issue ads. Recall that my category is "media" expenditures, which includes issue ads and *other* communication-related spending.

[26]The percentages are based on the assumption that all issue ads were funded exclusively with national party transfers. If state parties contributed money directly to the issue ads, then these percentages would be lower.

cess" soft money to increase traditional party activities. In 1996, spending on voter mobilization almost doubled from the previous presidential election, rising from $8 million to $16 million. Over the same period, spending on party hoopla activities increased sevenfold, from $1.2 to $8.3 million.

These figures are small in comparison to allocations for media-related activity. One reason is that the cost of bumper stickers, or even telephone banks, is considerably less than that of media-purchases in metropolitan markets. At about 10 cents per bumper sticker, one million dollars will purchase 10 million bumper stickers. The same amount will buy air time for about 40 ads (30 seconds) on network TV in a major media market during prime time.

It is important to note that media spending did not crowd out spending on traditional party activities. The portions of the party budget spent on mobilization and grassroots did not change substantially even when media spending soared. In the 1998 elections, Magleby (2000) reports that the parties, particularly the Democrats, emphasized a ground war strategy that involved lots of direct mail, telephone banks, and other get-out-the-vote activities. It appears, according to Table 2, that parties used additional soft money in 1998 to intensify mobilization efforts, spending nearly the same portion of their budget on such activities as they did in 1992 and 1994.

They used additional soft money to expand party headquarter operations. In 1992, state parties spent $42 million on overhead. By 1998, this had risen to $107 million. Certainly, one would want to know the degree to which these rising expenses at headquarters reflect sustained organizational growth or temporary surges in activity for the limited campaign season. A preliminary analysis of party budgets during the off-election year suggests that parties, especially the Republicans, made enduring investments in organization that expanded the party bureaucracy, even during the noncampaign season (La Raja 1999).

Partisan Differences?

The parties appear to spend similar amounts on all activities except for media. In 1996 the Democratic state parties allocated about $48 million for media, three times as much as the Republicans. The gap for the 1998 midterm election was not as great since neither party spent as much on media, but the Democratic state parties continued to outspend the Republicans at the state level by more than six million. These partisan differences exist because national Democrats, being the relatively poorer party, attempt to exploit soft money for federal races more than Republicans. They do this by transferring soft money to state parties where the spending ratios for soft and hard money are higher, meaning state parties can use more soft money than national parties to pay for the same activity.

Conclusion

Soft Money Contributions

My findings confirm some of the conventional wisdom about the potential problems with soft money contributions but raise interesting questions about the dominance of super donors and partisan biases in the system. Data from the elections of 1998 demonstrate that the average soft money donation is not as large as one might expect, given the news media's focus on the very largest donations. In fact, the *median* soft money donor gives a total of $500 (the value at which half the cases fall above and half below) and the *mode* (the most frequently occurring contribution) is only $250.[27] Preliminary data from other elections suggest that these estimates of central tendency have not risen substantially in the past decade.

The overwhelming number of small soft money donors explains why the average soft money contribution is so low, even though frequent news stories on campaign finance lead us to believe that the average is much higher. What this means is that a large pool of donors are participating at levels that are hardly corruption-prone. At a time when Americans appear to use their tax forms less and less to provide public funds for the presidential elections—only one in eight taxpayers now checks the public funding box—we cannot ignore the importance of providing candidates with relatively "clean" sources of money.[28] A ban on soft money would eliminate these valuable political resources for the parties and their candidates.[29] It might be wiser to put a reasonable cap on size of soft money contributions rather than abolish it entirely.

I also investigated the potential partisan advantages of the soft money system. Given the strength of Republican fundraising, their natural affinity with

---

[27]Median and mode are measures of central tendency, which are not as sensitive to extreme low and high values as the mean.

[28]Herbert Alexander, "Spending in the 1996 Election," in John C Green, ed., *Financing the 1996 Elections* (Armonk, N.Y.: M. E. Sharpe, 1999).

[29]The preponderance of small soft money donors makes one wonder why contributors give soft money rather than hard money if the amount they give is well within federal regulations. A likely answer is that these contributors have already "maxed out" with hard money contributions, and they want to contribute more through soft money. This is an empirical question worth exploring. If this does not explain the behavior of all contributors one might ask whether regulatory burdens impose costs on donors or parties that incline them to forego hard money in favor of soft money contributions. These costs might include paperwork or publicity that donors would rather avoid. The FEC requires parties to itemize soft and hard money contributors above $200. A donor might retain her anonymity by giving below $200 in hard money and below $200 in soft money. There may, of course, be other burdens of publicity associated with giving hard money donations that I am not aware of.

business, and their majority status in Congress, they apparently benefit more from soft money. This finding would explain their resistance to current reform efforts. The Democrats, by contrast, rely less on cash because they receive considerable in-kind support from labor organizations that conduct their own campaign operations. With public opinion polls favoring a ban, Democrats appear to benefit more than Republicans by pursuing legislation to ban soft money.

Democrats have always lagged far behind Republicans in hard money receipts, and they raise and spend soft money as a strategy to catch up.[30] The fact that the average soft money donation to Democrats is larger than to Republicans suggests that Democrats try to make up for a smaller donor base by capturing larger contributions. Seeking to wear the mantle of reform, Democrats may acquiesce to a soft money ban because they believe they can compete more evenly with Republicans in raising hard money, and they know they will continue to benefit from labor's in-kind activities. Democrats know that the longer the Republicans control Congress, the less business interests will be concerned about hedging their bets by giving to both parties. And now that the Republicans control the White House and its formidable fundraising advantages, it is reasonable to expect even more Democrats to favor a ban on soft money.

A ban on soft money could disadvantage Republicans since unions will continue to support Democratic candidates through in-kind services and campaigning. If there were a ban, it would not be surprising to see Republican party leaders develop strategies to institutionalize nonparty campaign activities among allied organizations, even though few Republican groups have the structural advantages for contacting members that labor unions possess.

Finally, there is the question of who benefits from donating party soft money? Although it is extremely difficult to demonstrate *quid pro quo* exchanges between contributors and elected officials let us assume, for argument's sake, that a dollar contribution is worth a dollar in benefits to the donor. Based on this analysis, it appears that business interests benefit from a soft money regime that allows them to offset the organizational advantages of labor organizations simply by providing cash to political parties.

Other groups contribute to the parties but nothing close to the levels provided by business or individual donors. I suspect that some of these groups increasingly favor the labor strategy of providing in-kind benefits to parties through issue ads or member contacts. Given this trend and the current legal environment framed by *Buckley v. Valeo,* it is likely that ideological and other nonparty organizations will gain influence in electoral politics if soft money is banned. The funding sources having been identified, it is unlikely political entrepreneurs will ignore the donor lists. They simply need to design methods to get these resources into selected campaigns.

---

[30]Brooks Jackson, *Honest Graft* (Washington, D.C.: Farragut Publishing, 1990 revised edition).

Soft Money Spending

Parties use soft money in ways that would strike many observers—including those favoring a ban on soft money—as positive. This preliminary study illustrates that parties use soft money to promote party building and citizen participation. If soft money permits the party to reach additional voters through telephone calls and mail, or generate enthusiasm for political campaigns through rallies and yard signs, then perhaps proposed reforms are shortchanging American campaigns by cutting off this money. The heavy emphasis on media strategies in the press and by public interest advocates obscures the fact that parties do many things with soft money.

Parties do exploit soft money to fund issue ads through state organizations. Media-related spending by state parties jumped from just $2 million in 1992 to $65 million in 1996. Democrats appear to use a state-sponsored issue ad strategy more than Republicans, probably because they trail Republicans in raising hard money. Both parties use most of their soft money to expand party headquarter operations during campaigns. From 1992 to 1998, they more than doubled the amount spent contacting individual voters through various voter identification and get-out-the-vote programs. In the last midterm election 16 percent of soft money went to issue ads, the same amount that was spent on direct mobilization and grassroots efforts.

If only a modest portion of party soft money goes to fund issue ads, it is worth re-examining the question: how is soft money harmful? The obvious answer is it permits candidates, contributors, and parties to circumvent federal laws limiting campaign contributions. If party soft money can help a specific candidate, then corporations, unions, or wealthy individuals can simply funnel contributions to candidates through the parties. And the potential for a *quid pro quo* exchange between contributor and policymaker escalates with the size of the contribution.

But assume for a moment that party money is "clean." Suppose it is generated through public subsidies, or raised from contributors in increments that are small enough to prevent corrupt exchanges. Are the spending patterns of parties harmful? Parties spend a significant portion of their cash to build the party as intended by the 1979 amendments to the FECA. Through soft money parties have access to resources that permit them to engage in activities that are, for the most part, salutary for the electoral system (see Ansolabehere and Snyder 2000). If solving the problem of corruption requires a ban on soft money, then reformers should find ways to ensure that parties have sufficient resources so they continue to occupy a central role in campaigns.

Earlier reforms in 1974 weakened the party's role in campaigns by institutionalizing PACs as legitimate contributors to candidate campaigns. PACs proliferated in the 1970s and early 1980s, providing an increasing share of candidate campaign funds. Candidates came to rely more on PACs than on parties, which encouraged candidate-centered campaigns. Ever adaptable, parties exploited campaign finance regulations to reestablish themselves. Soft money helped restore the party role in campaigns, making candidates less reliant on PACs. Party leaders may now feel beholden to big soft money contributors, a potential problem that should not be overlooked. If the soft money regime encourages interest groups to contribute more frequently through the party leadership, then soft money may simply centralize a corrupt exchange among powerful political actors.

I conclude with a policy recommendation that parties retain access to sufficient campaign resources to continue the activities they now pursue with soft money. My findings suggest that soft money encourages party building and party integration, much as Congress desired when it passed amendments to the campaign finance laws in 1979. To reduce the potential for corruption, I recommend that Congress place a cap on soft money contributions or, if soft money is banned, raise the limits on hard money contributions. The latter is a second best solution because the distinction between soft and hard money is still valuable. Soft money provides an incentive for national parties to transfer funds to state and local parties, where campaign activities have increased substantially. Grassroots work is enhanced at lower party levels that afford more opportunities for amateurs and volunteers to participate. National parties may be reluctant to transfer hard money to state parties for party building when they can use it themselves for direct candidate support and issue ads.

What is the appropriate amount to cap soft money? I would suggest a $100,000 limit on soft money contributions. This policy addresses several problems I raised earlier. First, it reduces the potential for corruption by eliminating the super donors, the one percent who give more than $100,000. Second, parties retain control of campaign resources, some of which support activities that encourage participation, such as voter mobilization and grassroots programs. More importantly, party control of these resources reduces the potential for campaigns to be dominated by outside groups waging independent campaigns. And voters will be able to link party activities with candidates more clearly than with independent actors who get involved in the campaign.

Finally, the $100,000 threshold addresses the realities of partisan politics. Republicans are unlikely to accede to a ban on soft money when they know that Democrats still benefit from labor unions' formidable support. And Democrats will fear raising the hard money contribution limits because they know Republicans have more hard money contributors, many of whom could afford to make larger contributions to the Republican party. Allowing parties to raise cash through soft money acknowledges the concerns of both parties and provides a basis for compromise that encourages partisan equity in the campaign finance system.

References

Alexander, Herbert E. 1999. "Spending in the 1996 Elections." In Financing the 1996 Election, ed. John C. Green. Armonk, N.Y.: M. E. Sharpe.

———— 1979. Financing the 1976 Election. Washington, D.C.: Congressional Quarterly.

American Political Science Association. 1950. Toward a More Responsible Two-Party System. New York: Rinehart.

Ansolabehere, Stephen, and James Snyder. 2000. "Soft Money, Hard Money, Strong Parties." 100 Columbia Law Review 3: 598–619.

Biersack, Robert. 1996. "The Nationalization of Party Finances." In The State of the Parties, ed. John C. Green and Daniel M. Shea. Lanham: M.D.: Rowman and Littlefield.

Broder, John M. 2000. "California Group Attacks Gore." The New York Times, National Edition, March 29.

Bureau of Labor Statistics. 2000. "Table 1. Consumer Price Index for All Urban Consumers (CPI-U): U.S. City Average, by expenditure category and commodity and service group," at http://stats.bls.gov/news.release/cpi.t01.htm.

Cain, Bruce E., and Dan Lowenstein. 1990. "Can Campaign Finance Reform Create a More Ethical Political Process?" Public Affairs Report, vol. 31, no. 1. Berkeley: Institute of Governmental Studies.

Chinoy, Ira, and Dan Morgan. 1997. "DNC Channeled Donations to State Parties, Washington Post, January 26.

Committee for the Study of the American Electorate. 1996. Use of Media Principal Reason Campaign Costs Skyrocket. Washington, D.C.: Committee for the Study of the American Electorate.

Committee for Economic Development. 1999. Investing in the People's Business: A Business Proposal for Campaign Finance Reform. N.Y.: Committee for Economic Development.

Corrado, Anthony. 1997. "Party Soft Money." In Campaign Finance Reform: A Sourcebook, Anthony Corrado et al., 165–77. Washington, D.C.: Brookings Institution.

————. 1993. Paying for Presidents. New York: Twentieth Century Fund.

Direct Marketing Association. 2000. Statistical Fact Book 1999. N.Y.: DMI.

Drew, Elizabeth. 1997. Whatever It Takes. N.Y.: Viking.

Dwyre, Diana. 1996. "Spinning Straw into Gold: Soft Money and U.S. House Elections." Legislative Studies Quarterly, vol. 21 (no. 3): 409–44.

FECinfo. 1998. "Soft Money Summary." December 28, at http://www.tray.com/ cgi-win/_smrpt.exe.

Federal Election Commission. 1978. Advisory Opinion 1978–10, "Allocation of Costs for Voter Registration."

————. 1995. Advisory Opinion 1995–25, "Costs of Advertising to Influence Congressional Legislation Allocated to Both Federal and Nonfederal Funds."

_____. 1999. "FEC Releases Information on PAC Activity for 1997–98." Press Release, June 8, 1999 at http://www.fec.gov/press/paccln98.htm.

_____. 1999. "FEC Reports on Political Party Activity for 1997–98." Press Release, April 9, 1999 at http://www.fec.gov/press/ptyye98.htm.

Heard, Alexander. 1960. The Costs of Democracy. Chapel Hill: University of North Carolina.

Herrnson, Paul. 1988. Party Campaigning in the 1980s. Cambridge: Harvard University.

Isikoff, Michael. 2000. "The Secret Money Chase." Newsweek, June 5.

Jackson, Brooks. 1990. Honest Graft. Revised edition. Washington, D.C.: Farragut Publishing.

Jacobson, Gary C. 1980. Money in Congressional Elections. New Haven: Yale University.

Joe, Wesley, and Clyde Wilcox. 1999. "Financing the 1996 Presidential Nominations: The Last Regulated Campaign?" In Financing the 1996 Election, ed. John Green. Armonk, N.Y.: Sharpe, 37–62.

Kayden, Xandra, and Eddie Mahe, Jr. 1985. The Party Goes On. N.Y.: Basic Books.

Kosterlitz, Julie. 1996. "Firing Back at Labor." National Journal, March 26, p. 474.

Krasno, Jonathan, and Daniel E. Seltz. 2000. Buying Time: Television Advertising in the 1998 Congressional Elections. N.Y.: Brennan Center for Justice at NYU School of Law.

La Raja, Raymond J. 1999. "The Impact of Soft Money on State Party Behavior: Do Soft Money Transfers Increase the Size of the Party Organization?" Prepared for delivery at the 1999 annual meeting of the American Political Science Association, Atlanta Marriott Marquis and Atlanta Hilton and Towers, September 2–5.

Magleby, David, ed. 2000. Outside Money: Soft Money and Issue Advocacy in the 1998 Congressional Elections. N.Y.: Rowman and Littlefield.

Sorauf, Frank J. 1992. Inside Campaign Finance. New Haven: Yale University.

VandeHei, Jim. 2000. "Gun-control Efforts Trigger Strong NRA Drive for GOP." The Wall Street Journal, May 5, A18.

Van Natta, Jr., Don. 2000. "As Political Gifts Set a Record Pace, Some Quit Giving." The New York Times, May 2.

Verba, Sidney, Kay Lehman Schlozman, and Henry E. Brady. 1995. Voice and Equality: Civic Voluntarism in American Politics. Cambridge: Harvard University Press.

Chapter 6

Contributing as Political Participation

Clyde Wilcox

Contributing to parties, candidates, and interest groups is one way that Americans participate in politics. Individuals may legally give directly to candidates at the national, state, and local level, and to political parties and interest groups that support candidates. Individuals may also spend their own money independently to advocate the election of candidates. The Federal Election Commission Act (FECA) regulates contributing and spending in national elections; state law regulates giving in state and local elections.

Frank Sorauf (1988) estimates that two to four million Americans gave money to congressional candidates in 1984. That figure has doubtlessly risen over time, and when presidential, state, and local candidates are included the figure might approach eight million. Whatever the total, contributing is a rare form of political participation. Most Americans do not give, and those who do have distinctive socio-economic profiles and policy views.

As we contemplate reforms to the campaign finance system, it is helpful to consider giving as a form of participation, and to assess its benefits and harms to democratic governance. This chapter considers the implications of the participatory aspect of campaign contributions and discusses some advantages and disadvantages of reform proposals that view giving as participation. Rather than offer my "ideal" reforms of a campaign finance system, I will focus on those that might logically flow from the participatory aspects of giving. Finally, I will suggest some avenues for future research that might help us better understand this aspect of contributing.

Giving as Participation

Two questions arise if we consider campaign giving as a form of participation. First, there are the possible positive consequences of political giving—for individuals, for politics, and for democracy. Participation, it is argued, enhances the democratic capacities of individuals, provides for more public deliberation, and gives citizens a feeling they have a stake in the political system. If contributing creates these positive effects, then reforms should seek to increase the number of Americans who contribute.

Second, we must consider the effects of unequal participation in financing elections. Only half of Americans vote, an even smaller number is active in political groups, and giving is rarer still. Campaigns rely on a small number of active donors for the bulk of their money. If candidates and policymakers are more likely to listen to donors, and if donors have views on public policy issues that are different from nondonors, then the democratic process may be distorted by the unequal voice of those who have the most money to give. In this case, reforms should seek to curb the disproportionate voice of donors.

Contribution as Positive Participation

Participation carries a positive connotation, with the implied notion that the more active the public, the better it is for democracy. There are many types of participation, and some individuals appear to specialize in different modes of participation—working in campaigns, community activity, and contacting government about personal problems (Verba and Nie 1972). These activities require different resources, and may have different effects on those who participate.

Warren (2000) argues that through activity in voluntary associations people become more interested in politics, have more confidence in their political abilities, become better informed and more skillful citizens. It may be that giving has similar effects. Putnam (1993) argues that polities with citizenry that participates actively in civic and political organizations are better able to govern.

Yet Warren also argues that involvement in some groups does not enhance democratic capabilities, nor enable better public deliberation, because these groups focus on exclusive group identity or particularistic benefits. Clearly some political participation entails different types of activity than others and thus might have different effects on individuals. Canvassing a neighborhood for a candidate requires interacting and speaking with fellow citizens. Membership in a voluntary association with face-to-face meetings and a contended issue agenda requires verbal and political skills to build arguments and coalitions (Mansbridge 1995). Giving money requires, in its sparest form, merely writing a check, and might be less likely to lead to positive democratic effects among participants.

Does giving enhance individual capacities for democratic politics? We know little about the long-term effects of giving, for there has been little empirical work. We do know that giving, like voting, is a habit, and that most donors are part of an enduring donor pool that exists across election cycles and across different types of campaigns (Brown, Powell, and Wilcox 1996; Francia, Green, Herrnson, Powell, and Wilcox 2001). The most active donors give routinely to all types of campaigns, while others give in some elections but not others, or only to a particular type of candidate. The most active donors have different social and political characteristics than less active donors—they hold stronger party identification and ideological views, for example—but this may be the source, not the result, of their greater level of giving.

The donor pool changes gradually over time, as some donors leave the pool and others join it. Some enter because of a personal solicitation from a friend or business associate that they do not wish to refuse. Others enter because a candidate or cause interests them—Jesse Jackson mobilized African Americans in 1984, Pat Robertson appealed to charismatic Christians in 1988, and Elizabeth Dole recruited contributions from Republican women in 2000. Yet even these mobilizations were mostly among those who had given in the past. Among donors to Pat Robertson in 1988, for example, only six percent had never given to a presidential candidate, although half had never given to Senate or congressional candidates. Two thirds of the new donors to Robertson in 1988 gave to a different candidate in 1992, suggesting that those who enter the donor pool usually stay.

New donors stay, in part, because candidates solicit their contributions. George Bush in 1992 solicited nearly every donor who had given to any Republican candidate in 1988; Patrick Buchanan rented and solicited Jack Kemp's donor list (Brown, et al. 1995). Major fundraisers in presidential campaigns sign up for new candidates four years later and solicit their network on behalf of their new patron. For some Americans a single gift to an inspiring candidate gathered by a persuasive solicitor can lead to a lifetime of giving.

But we do not know the effect on citizens of becoming a contributor. Does increased involvement in the donor pool change the capacities or attitudes of citizens? Do donors become more interested or informed about politics, more efficacious, more tolerant? In the absence of hard data, we might speculate on some of the effects posited by Warren and others: interest in politics, information, efficacy, political skills, and civic virtues such as tolerance. Future research on this question would be useful in determining the value of contributing as a form of participation.

We begin with the assumption that many characteristics of donors—their education, income, and many of their attitudes and skills—were acquired prior to the time of their first contribution. We are therefore interested in change in attitudes and orientations that accompanies the process of joining and becoming an active donor.

Contributing might increase interest in politics, but the effect is likely to be modest. In data from the National Election Studies from 1990 through 1998, givers were slightly more likely than nondonors to report an interest in politics. Yet this correlation does not tell us that giving actually causes interest—it is at least equally plausible that citizens interested in politics are more likely to give money to candidates. It is possible that both occur: interested citizens are more likely to be enticed to give, and as a consequence become somewhat more interested in elections and politics. Much as an individual becomes more interested in a football game after placing a bet, donors may become more interested in particular races and candidates to which they have given. But individuals with the same levels of income and education as donors are already quite interested in politics, and it is likely that the impact of giving on interest is small.

Donors may become better informed about elections and policymaking as a result of their gifts. Party and congressional leaders meet with their most generous donors and brief them on competitive races and upcoming legislation. Donors to PACs and interest groups receive newsletters that detail issues of special importance to the group, and the positions of candidates on those issues. Surveys of donors in House and Senate elections show that members do respond to this information, often giving in accord with groups to which they are members (Francia, Green, Herrnson, Powell, and Wilcox 2001). Donors begin with significant amounts of information, but it is likely that giving makes them more informed.

Giving may increase donor's feelings of efficacy, since giving is associated with access. Indeed, surveys have shown that the efficacy of donors sometimes exceeds researcher expectations: in one survey of 1972 donors one woman penciled in an extra category to a question on local efficacy—saying that she "owned the town." It is also possible that some donors feel less efficacious over time: some of the soft money donors who testified in the Senate investigation of Clinton fundraising indicated that they believed that the threshold for true access was a larger amount that they had contributed.

Giving probably does little to enhance a donor's political skills, for unlike face-to-face politics, giving simply involves writing a check. Mingling with other donors at fundraising events may increase political and social skills, but people who can afford a ticket and are attracted by the benefits of such an event are likely to have significant skills already.

Finally, it is unlikely that giving increases the "civic virtues" of political tolerance and civility. Small donors who are solicited through the mail are routinely exposed to communications designed to inspire fear of their political opponents, and involvement in these networks of communications might actually decrease civic virtues. Attending large fundraising dinners does sometimes expose donors to others with somewhat different policy proposals and even party attachments, but these social occasions are unlikely to have much influence on political tolerance or support for the rules of the game.

Donors come from an elite already interested in politics, already informed about the political process, already efficacious, skilled, and more tolerant of diversity than the average American. The process of becoming more active in giving may increase a donor's information and interest, but does little to increase other democratic capacities. It might be that the effects of giving would be somewhat different if those with lower levels of interest, information, and efficacy were recruited to the donor pool. Yet giving seems especially isolated from the kinds of interpersonal interactions that are most likely to affect individual democratic capacities.

If giving only modestly increases democratic capacities, it might have other benefits. It may help link citizens to candidates and constituencies to officeholders, and thus increase a feeling of a stake in the system. Giving networks may create a space to discuss issues and aggregate positions. These systemic effects might suggest reforms that would stimulate giving among those normally not part of the donor pool.

Clearly some donors establish strong links to the candidates they support. Those who give serious money to incumbents often establish personal relationships to candidates. The social occasions where large contributions are made often create an atmosphere that fosters personal and political connections.

But most small donors are linked to candidates through intermediary groups. Those who give to Emily's List, for example, constitute a financial constituency for pro-choice women candidates, and incumbents who receive money from the group sometimes provide special communications to group members who gave to their campaign. There is some evidence that this occurs for donors of smaller amounts as well. In 1988, a significant portion of donors to Pat Robertson's presidential campaign—many of whom gave $200 or less—indicated that they knew the candidate personally. Robertson's campaign finance director suggested to me that few of these donors actually knew the candidate, but the process of giving to him coupled with watching his *700 Club* television show, created a close bond between donor and candidate.

The more important systemic effect of giving would occur if giving increased an individual's belief that they have a stake in the system—an affective evaluation that might increase system legitimacy, trust in government, and a commitment to work toward better social and political policies. In the NES data from 1990 through 1998, those who give to candidates, parties, or PACs are not more trusting of government, nor are they less or more likely to believe that the government is run by a few big interests. It might be that those who give larger sums are more distinctive in these attitudes, but we lack data. Thus giving does not appear to increase attachment to or trust in government, although the evidence is not definitive for larger contributors.

What is clear is that the current system of campaign finance increases cynicism and distrust of government. Currently, surveys show that a majority of Americans believe that the political system is corrupted by big money, and that wealthy donors have disproportionate influence. A survey by Princeton Survey Research Associates conducted for the Center for Responsive Politics showed that a majority of Americans think that at least most campaigns use "questionable fundraising practices—breaking or bending the rules about how money can be raised." Table 6.1 shows selected responses to this survey.

A majority of respondents believe that access to the president was sold for political contributions, that those who give want something from government, that contributions prevent passage of legislation that would help ordinary citizens, that political candidates vote against citizen interests in exchange for contributions, and that political money makes elected officials less likely to care what average citizens say (www.opensecrets.org/pubs/survey/s1.html). Although the survey design might lead to an overstatement of negative views on campaign finance, the overwhelming numbers of citizens who express these views suggest that attitudes toward the campaign finance system lower legitimacy of government (Joe and Wilcox 2000).

Whether the public indictment of the campaign finance system is accurate is unclear; what matters is that the system of private financing does not appear to raise trust among donors, and is a source of distrust among nondonors (see also Hibbing and Theis-Morse 1997). There is considerable belief among the public that the government is unduly influenced by donors, and this contributes to their distrust of government in general and of Congress in particular.

One final potential benefit from private contributions is that giving networks might create spaces in which political deliberation can occur, where issues are debated and discussed, and candidate preferences developed. This "discussion" might be indirect—individuals who receive newsletters and mail solicitations from Emily's List might become involved in a debate over whether all Democratic pro-choice women are worth supporting, or whether candidates must also show support for a broader feminist or progressive agenda. Direct mail from the Christian Coalition might inspire debate in the family or church about which issues have a religious base and which are purely secular. Fundraising dinners might provide the opportunity for constituencies to discuss and debate political issues.

There is little evidence on this question, but it is unlikely that much serious deliberation occurs as a result of contributions. The scholarship on direct mail stresses not its deliberative value but its highly emotional appeals and heated

Table 6.1. Citizen Attitudes on Campaign Finance

Question	Percent
Questionable fundraising in most campaigns	75%
Questionable fundraising affects country's domestic policy at least some	73%
Access to the president seemed to be sold in exchange for contributions	78%
Money is sometimes used to stop legislation for average citizens	89%
Money sometimes leads elected officials to vote against their constituent's interests	89%
Money sometimes gives one group more influence	91%
Money makes elected officials not care what average citizens think	71%

Source: Princeton Survey Research Associates survey for Center for Responsive Politics

rhetoric. Such solicitations typically portray opposition groups or political figures as dangerous, anti-American, and worthy of defeat. There has been little research on the persuasive value of these communications, and I think some of them do provoke some conversation within families and friendship networks, but the true deliberative value of these discussions is relatively low. Similarly, fundraising events do inspire some discussion of politics, but differences are usually suppressed in favor of a portrayal of similarities, and these events play at most a modest deliberative role.

In sum, although there is little hard data on these questions, it seems likely that giving has some modest positive effects, primarily in increasing the information and interest of an already advantaged political elite, and giving networks may have slightly positive or moderately negative effects on political deliberation, depending on the nature of the appeal.

This discussion has uncovered one strongly negative effect: many Americans believe that donors get special access and influence on policies, and that the system by which candidates raise money from individuals and groups gives some Americans more voice than others. These results provide at best only weak support for reforms that would expand the donor pool to include new individuals, many of whom may lack information and interest in campaigns.

116   Clyde Wilcox

Contributing and Participatory Distortion

If contributing has modest positive consequences for individuals and society, it may also have some negative consequences. Giving may be an additional source of political inequality, expanding the political voice of the advantaged and channeling a distorted image of public opinion into government institutions.

All political participation requires certain resources. Voting requires time to gather at least some information, cognitive skills to form judgment, and the ability to cast a ballot. Participation in political groups requires time, verbal and social skills, and some financial resources. Contributing requires some thought, but it mainly requires substantial financial resources. A contribution of $25 may be a significant investment for many families, whereas a contribution of $20,000 may be of little consequence for others.

Verba, Schlozman, and Brady (1995) note that among major modes of political participation, giving is unique in that it requires little in the way of social and cognitive resources. In a major study of voluntary activity in politics and society, they found that only three factors predict giving among political activists, and by far the most important is wealth. They conclude, "in comparison to modes of participation based on giving time, modes of participation based on giving money are especially worrisome from the perspective of political equality" (28). Free time is distributed relatively evenly among Americans across class, race, and gender lines, but money is not. Moreover, the maximum amount of time anyone can give to a candidate or cause is limited by the number of hours in a day and by other demands on that time (e.g., to eat and sleep, and perhaps to work for wages). The maximum amount of soft money an individual can give, or spend on issue advocacy, is limited only by his resources. Thus in giving, there is a great skew in the availability of the resources needed for participation, and an even greater skew in the actual level of the activity.

Verba et al. argue that differential rates of political participation can cause participatory distortion when the government hears only a limited set of voices. They report that there is sizable distortion on economic attitudes and income in all forms of participation, but that distortion is seriously troubling in the case of giving. Because affluent donors are more conservative than the average American on economic issues, if elected policymakers listen primarily to their voices, they hear a distinctive subset of Americans. The authors conclude that giving produces significant participatory distortion, despite the fact that the average contribution in their study was less than $75. Even at these small amounts, donors have very different attitudes than those who do not give, and if government listens to givers it does not hear a representative voice of America.

My own analysis of data from the National Election Studies supports these conclusions. Between nine percent and 11 percent of respondents indicate that they have given to one or more campaign finance actors—candidates, parties, or

PACs—in each year since 1990. Nearly 33 percent of those in the top five percent of income gave, but only four percent of those in the bottom 17 percent on the income scale contributed. Donors differ on other characteristics as well—they have higher levels of education and are more interested in politics, for example. But income is the single best predictor of giving in politics. Giving does not increase steadily with income; the very wealthy are far more likely to give than even middle-class citizens. Giving increases only incrementally among those in the bottom 66 percent of income, and is sharply higher among those in the top five percent. Indeed, once the indirect effects of income are considered, the wealthiest five percent are more than seven times more likely to give as the least affluent citizens.[1] The wealthiest Americans are more likely to participate in other ways as well. They are more than twice as likely to vote than the least affluent Americans, for example, but their distinctiveness on giving is much greater.

Their disproportionate rate of giving is especially important because donors have special access to policymakers. In the NES data, those who gave to candidates and to either a party or a PAC were nearly three times as likely as those who did not give to contact their member of Congress. Of course, given their wealth, income, and interest in politics, donors might be more likely to contact members of Congress even if they do not give. Yet my analysis of the NES data suggests that donors are significantly more likely to contact members of Congress than others who share their income, education, and interest in politics. Among the best-educated citizens, for example, donors are twice as likely to contact a member of Congress as a nondonor. Among the smaller set of those with highest income, education, and interest in campaigns, donors are 40 percent more likely to contact their representative as nondonors.[2]

This disproportionate voice carries a distinctive set of policy preferences. Wealthy citizens are more conservative than other Americans on economic issues, and donors are even more conservative than wealthy nondonors. My analysis of NES data shows that donors are significantly more conservative than other wealthy and well-educated citizens on economic issues—guaranteed jobs, spending on social programs, affirmative action—but not on social issues such as women's roles or abortion, or on foreign policy. This analysis confirms findings that participatory distortion from giving is especially high on economic issues.

Donors have a distinctive set of policy preferences and are much more likely than other Americans to contact Congress to voice their positions. The

---

[1]This considers the indirect effects of income on interest and strength of partisanship, holding constant education.

[2]Of course, this correlation is probably the result of two processes. Donors doubtlessly get more access, but those who contact members of Congress may be more likely to be solicited for contributions, and possibly to give money in turn.

participatory distortion is actually understated in these data because most of the donors in the NES give only small amounts. Those who give the largest contributions provide most of the money in American elections and have an even stronger voice in politics and policymaking.

The NES does not allow us to determine how much individuals give, but Verba et al. report an average contribution among donors of $75. The average total contributed rose to more than $200 only among those with incomes approaching $50,000. Contributions of $200 get more notice by candidates and policymakers; they are reported to the Federal Election Commission in national races, and to state electoral commissions in many states. Thus participatory distortion may be even greater if those who give larger contributions hold even more distinctive views.

One survey of donors to congressional campaigns in 1996 revealed that donors of $200 or more are far wealthier than those who give smaller amounts. Table 6.2 shows the demographic profile of this group (Biersack, Herrnson, Powell, and Wilcox 2001). The study included a random sample of all donors who gave at least $200, and this sample has been divided into Occasional Donors, who give only in some elections, and Habitual Donors, who give in most elections to congressional candidates. The column that identified the Most Active Donors is from a separate survey of donors who gave $8,000 total contributions, or contributions of $200 or more to eight or more candidates. In 1998, approximately 2/3 of the money raised by House and Senate candidates came in amounts of $200 or more, so clearly this group of donors dominates the campaign finance system.

This table shows that donors of larger amounts are far wealthier than the more typical smaller donors identified by Verba, et al. Three quarters of those who give $200 or more have incomes of $100,000 or greater, and a majority of the most active donors have incomes of more than $500,000. They are disproportionately male, white, older, well educated, and more likely to be mainline Protestants or Jews and less likely to be evangelical Christians. In each case, the bias in the overall donor pool is magnified among those who give larger sums. Our survey included a number of donors who gave "soft money" to political parties. More than 97 percent of this money came from donors with annual incomes of more than $500,000.

These donors of larger amounts have significant access to politicians. Nearly 60 percent of habitual donors have contacted more than two House members and more than two senators in the past two years. More than a quarter of the most active donors have contacted 11 or more members of the House, and 11 or more senators. Two-thirds of the most active donors know their representative personally. For the most active contributors, access is not occasional; they have ready access to multiple members. Whereas average citizens voice their preferences at the ballot box or in a letter to their member, active donors can talk personally with members and their staff whenever they need or want. More than

Table 6.2. Characteristics of the Donors of Larger Amounts

	Occasional Donors	Habitual Donors	Most Active Donors
Education:			
High School -	4%	5%	1%
College	25%	2%	29%
Some Graduate+	55%	64%	64%
Income:			
$99k -	25%	19%	4%
$100k-$499k	63%	65%	45%
$500k+	12%	15%	52%
Religion:			
Mainline Prot	35%	47%	32%
Evang Prot	14%	10%	5%
Catholics	28%	19%	12%
Jews	11%	11%	39%
Secular/Other	12%	14%	11%
Age:			
18–30	1%	1%	1%
31–45	23%	12%	6%
46–60	42%	42%	39%
61+	35%	45%	54%
Male	72%	82%	77%
White	99%	99%	99%

[1]This considers the indirect effects of income on interest and strength of partisanship, holding constant education.
[2]Of course, this correlation is probably the result of two processes. Donors doubtlessly get more access, but those who contact members of Congress may be more likely to be solicited for contributions, and possibly to give money in turn.

2/3 have spoken directly with the member of Congress in the past two years about a policy issue that concerned them, an even larger number have spoken with directly with congressional staff,

These data are not surprising to anyone who follows closely the financing of American elections. Solicitations to fundraising events that require significant contributions (and especially to soft-money fundraisers) often carry with them a promise of access. The timing of congressional fundraisers has increasingly coincided with major congressional markups, with the implicit assumption that the donor will want access at that time.

Once again this extra access comes with a distinctive policy tilt—the most active donors tend to be moderate on social issues but quite conservative on economic policy. Pluralities took conservative positions on all economic issues in the survey, from tax cuts to health care to the environment. A plurality even opposed "doing more to reduce poverty," a phrasing that typically gets strong support in the general public. Although differences in question wording makes inference tentative, it appears that donors of larger amounts are even more distinctive on economic issues than those who make the more modest contributions that were the average in the Verba et al. study.

Taken together, these data and earlier studies suggest that contributing is a form of participation that produces distortion by giving disproportionate access and voice to a wealthy elite that is able and willing to make sizable contributions to candidates, parties, and groups. These data do not show that donors receive more policy attention than other citizens, or that they get any real policy payoffs for their money. And the data do not prove that members of Congress listen only to donors.

Most casework by House members is done for constituents, for example, and not out-of-district donors, and most senators and members respond to mail from their constituents. Yet within districts, my analysis of NES data shows that donors are much more likely than nondonors to contact members of Congress to express their opinion. And donors believe that contributors seek favors from government—more than half believe that donors pressure policymakers for favors.

Donors and Campaign Finance Reform

How do donors feel about participating in the campaign finance system? Our survey of congressional donors revealed great ambivalence among those who finance congressional elections (Wilcox, Francia, Green, Herrnson, and Powell 2000). Nearly four in five believe that giving is a legitimate form of participation, but there was significant unhappiness with the current system. Fully 76 percent believe that the campaign finance system needs major changes, or to be replaced. A large majority of donors believe that officeholders regularly pressure donors for money, and more than half believe that donors pressure officeholders for favors.

There was substantial support among donors for several key reforms. More than three in four favored banning soft money and a significant majority supported spending limits and limits on television advertising. Other reforms divided donors, with Democrats favoring public funding and Republicans opposing such reforms. Yet the dissatisfaction among donors themselves suggests that it might be possible to craft reforms that address giving as a form of participation.

Implications for Reform

The two analyses discussed above yield two different avenues of reform. If giving increases democratic capacities, even slightly, among advantaged citizens, and if we believe that the effects might be even greater among those with lower levels of interest, efficacy, and skills, then reform should seek to expand the donor pool by encouraging a wider range of citizens to give. If giving provides a disproportionate voice for wealthy Americans and creates participatory distortion, then reforms should either decrease that voice or increase the voice of those who lack the money to give. The following discussion is not a coherent package of reforms, but rather an exploration of reforms that flow out of our consideration of giving as participation.

Expanding the Donor Pool

Increasing the donor pool might provide the advantages of giving to more citizens, and, if the pool's demographic profile changed, it might reduce participatory distortion as well. The 1974 reforms sought to increase the donor pool in presidential elections by limiting the size of contributions and by providing a public subsidy as an incentive to raise smaller gifts (matching funds). In both cases, the logic was that candidates would seek out new donors, often those willing to give smaller amounts. So one way to expand the donor pool is to create incentives for candidates to appeal to more contributors.

A comparison of the presidential donor pool between 1972 and 1988, however, found that although the number of donors had expanded, donors in 1988 were just as unrepresentative of the public as those in 1972 (Brown, Powell, and Wilcox 1995). Although candidates such as Jesse Jackson and Pat Robertson did expand the donor pool through appeals to less affluent citizens, they were balanced by the efforts of George Bush, Michael Dukakis, and others to appeal to nondonors similar to other large contributors—most likely their friends and neighbors. Even those who gave to Robertson and Jackson had average incomes substantially above the national median.

Contribution limits do not therefore appear to force candidates to expand the donor pool, and recent innovations in soft money and issue advocacy spending on behalf of campaigns make it even less likely that limits would do so in the future. Nor do incentives built into the matching fund system seem likely to lead future presidential candidates to court smaller donors. Bush and Gore could have raised more money in 2000 without matching funds than with them, and Bush's victory in the GOP primaries demonstrated that declining matching funds does not carry a political price. It may well be that most mainstream candidates of both parties will eschew matching funds in favor of unlimited spending in future campaigns, and court primarily $1,000 donors.

Changing the matching fund ratio to match only small contributions, or to match smaller donations at a 3–1 ratio, might induce candidates to solicit smaller donors, and matching funds might be adopted in congressional elections as well. Such reforms would have their own problems, including advantaging candidates with ideologically extreme views who can raise money via direct mail, but they would give candidates an incentive to solicit donations from a wider range of citizens. In contrast, reforms that might raise the maximum amount that an individual or group can give would decrease the need by candidates and parties to seek smaller contributions. A ban on soft money, on the other hand, would force parties to try to expand the donor pool to replace those large contributions. A combination—banning soft money and increasing the limits—would probably have little net effect on the number of Americans who give.

Reforms might simply try to encourage citizens to give to candidates, although reforms to encourage less affluent Americans to give have a poor track record. There is little evidence, for example, that tax deductions significantly widen the donor pool. Those Americans sufficiently alert to tax consequences itemize deductions and are wealthy enough to be in the donor pool. When the deduction for political contributions disappeared in 1986, it had no appreciable effect on giving.

One reform that might address both unequal benefits of giving and unequal voice would be a variant of public funding where citizens receive a contribution voucher from the government, which they can direct to the candidate, party, or group of their choice. Vouchers are preferable to tax deductions or credits, since the latter work only if individuals have sufficient income to give and understand the complexity of the income tax. A tax credit would be more politically palatable, although it would eliminate anyone who does not pay taxes from the donor base. Tax deductions are worth more for the wealthy (who are in a higher tax bracket) than for those of modest means, and are usually claimed only by those who file the "long form" on taxes.

A voucher system would solve two of the problems identified in this chapter—that the benefits of giving accrue only to advantaged citizens who have money to give, and that those who lack the resources to give have much less voice in policymaking. A modest voucher system would not equalize voice, but the collective power of a class of less affluent donors might give them greater voice in politics. Vouchers could be a ticket into the donor pool for some Americans who have the means to make modest contributions. Of course, public funding has other disadvantages and is not politically feasible at this time. Yet the potential political effects of parties and candidates competing for vouchers from all citizens are interesting and even amusing to contemplate.

Technology may enable campaigns to identify new sets of donors even without policy change. Direct mail and to a lesser extent telemarketing have given campaigns the capacity to tap into ideological Americans with significantly lower incomes than other donors. Internet fundraising is in its infancy, but it reportedly reaches a younger, more technologically sophisticated set of donors, perhaps those with less income. It might be that technology would merely catch donors earlier in their life cycle, before they had accumulated the wealth that brings invitations to dinners and events, but it could also be that the Internet would reach new demographic groups. Anecdotal evidence suggests that the Internet has been a source of donors who support campaign finance reform.

Decreasing the Value of Contributions

Another reform strategy would provide other resources to candidates, thereby devaluing the private contributions they receive by in essence inflating the currency. Public resources could come with strings attached—for example spending limits, or distributional fundraising limits—although these reforms have their own problems. Public funding of campaigns might go far to equalizing voices for all Americans, yet it is also possible that, freed from the necessity of asking for money, candidates would still spend their time among the political elites of their districts and states. Yet even if elections were publicly financed and private contributions banned, independent expenditures and issue advocacy would remain as outlets for political money, and even larger amounts would be channeled into these activities, lessening candidate control of campaigns. It might be possible to craft a public financing bill that would allow extra resources for those who face independent spending campaigns, but such a provision would be tricky at best and probably only partially effective.

A system of partial public funding—"floors without ceilings" might serve a similar function, as would free mailings or subsidized television or radio advertising. Subsidies could be created for candidates who raise a significant portion of their revenues in small contributions, but enforcement would require vigilance in an era of increasingly diverse noncandidate committees.

Yet despite any potentially salutary effects of public subsidies on candidate emergence and the diversity of the candidate pool, the effects on equality of voice would be modest, so long as private contributions or spending can be used to top off public money. Campaigns and parties have demonstrated an almost unlimited appetite for money in recent years, and if wealthy interests merely shift from contributions to issue advocacy, their voice would be somewhat diluted, but still disproportionately strong.

Banning or Limiting Soft Money

If soft money donors are especially unrepresentative, and if they have even greater access, then a ban or limit on soft money would curb some of the most egregious aspects of participatory distortion. Surveys show that a significant majority of both Republican and Democratic donors support such a ban, making this a policy around which a serious coalition could be built. Yet if soft money donors channeled their money instead into issue advocacy, the individuals and groups who made large soft money donations might find another route to greater access. Some argue that banning soft money will reduce the total funds spent on elections, which might hinder party communications. A soft money ban is more attractive if the hard money contribution limits are lifted to reflect inflation since 1974.

Banning soft money would help with the potentially serious problem that the public perceives political money to be a corrupting influence on politics that gives the rich control of politics. If Congress would shut off or reduce the flow of large contributions, it might take a modest step toward reestablishing trust in government and feelings of legitimacy among the American public. But if soft money is simply replaced by more hard money raised in the same types of fundraising events linked to committee markups, the longer-term effect on system legitimacy might be minimal.

Overall, considering giving as participation does not lead to a clear set of reform proposals. Yet it does focus our attention on the inequalities of privately financed elections, and help us to consider the implications of this inequality.

Implications for Future Research

There is much that we do not know about contributing as participation, and some of these questions might be answered with some well-focused research. We know little, for example, about the impact of giving on donors. Does the process of giving, and becoming involved in the networks of contacts and communications that follow, change an individual's capacities or orientations? I have speculated that these effects would be minimal and confined to a few areas, but we have little data on this question.

It would be most helpful to follow potential contributors as they enter the donor pool, to see how their beliefs and behaviors change. We have ready samples of such potential donors in studies such as Verba et al.'s survey of citizen activists, and it would be possible to follow these potential donors over time. Other types of local studies might help us more clearly understand any potential positive values of giving. The most interesting and elusive question is whether any of these benefits would accrue to individuals outside of the normal pool of donors—that is, individuals who may lack the education and social connections typical of donors.

We also know very little about what donors get for their money. Clearly donors get access, and the data I have presented here show that they get significantly more access than other constituents who share their education, income, and interest in politics. Yet we do not know whether they receive concrete policy benefits. This is likely to be a difficult question to answer, as decades of research on the impact of PAC contributions on congressional voting has demonstrated. Yet it is central to much of the argument about participatory distortion. If members of Congress hear from donors but also heed donor surveys and hear ordinary constituents in town meetings and visits to the district, and if members are able to mentally "weight" the views of donors, then unequal access may be less of a problem. If, on the other hand, members provide policy payoffs to donors, or if they give their views disproportionate weight, or even if their perception of district opinion is shaped by a narrower subset of in-district donors, then the distortion is an important problem for democracy.

One segment of this question that is most immediately amenable to research would be to see if members of Congress are more likely to be mistaken about the views of their district because they hear most from a disproportionate minority. It might be easiest to study this at the state and local level, where access to policymakers is easier.

As we ponder reform of campaign finance from many different perspectives, there is much that we do not know. Whatever reforms may finally pass, it will be important to chart their impact on individual donors as well as on the financial health of parties and interest groups. Participation is but one of many important windows through which to view this debate, but it raises interesting issues for those who seek to understand the workings of the system, and to craft reform.

References

Brown, Clifford, Lynda Powell, and Clyde Wilcox. 1996. *Serious Money: Contributing and Fundraising in Presidential Nomination Politics.* New York: Cambridge University Press.

Francia, Peter, John Green, Paul Herrnson, Lynda Powell, and Clyde Wilcox. 2001 (forthcoming). *Investors, Ideologues, and Intimates: Individual Donors in Congressional Elections.* New York: Columbia University Press.

Sorauf, Frank J. 1988. *Money in American Elections.* San Francisco: Scott Foresman.

Verba, Sidney, and Norman H. Nie. 1972. *Participation in America: Political Democracy and Social Equality.* New York: Harper and Row.

Verba, Sidney, Kay Lehman Schlozman, and Henry E. Brady. 1995. *Voice and Equality Civic Voluntarism in American Politics.* Cambridge, Mass.: Harvard University Press.

Warren, Mark. 2000. *Democracy and Association.* Princeton: Princeton University Press.

Chapter 7

Judges in the Political Thicket

E. Joshua Rosenkranz

Half a century ago, Justice Felix Frankfurter warned his colleagues on the Supreme Court to steer clear of the "political thicket."[1] Judges, he believed, were
ill-suited to muddle in the realm of politics. For one thing, the Constitution—
replete with open-ended phrases such as "equal protection," "freedom of
speech," and "Republican Form of Government"—offers judges little guidance
on how to resolve knotty political questions. Equally important, as the only un-
elected branch of government, the judiciary has no practical understanding of
how elections and political institutions work. What's more, litigation is a clumsy
instrument for assessing political science data and drawing rational conclusions
about politics, much less for predicting the likely impact of changes in legal
rules or structures. So, Justice Frankfurter warned, judges only invite mischief
when they assume the mantle of amateur political scientists and presume to re-
shape political institutions. As he put it, "It is hostile to a democratic system to
involve the judiciary in the politics of the people. And it is not less pernicious if

---

[1]*Colgrove v. Green,* 328 U.S. 549 (1946) (concluding that courts lack the authority
to consider challenges to apportionment schemes based upon the Guaranty Clause); *see
also Baker v. Carr,* 369 U.S. 186 (1962) (Frankfurter, J., dissenting) (objecting to the
Court's decision to enter the political fray by permitting judicial review of apportionment
schemes under the Equal Protection Clause).

such judicial intervention in an essentially political contest be dressed up in the abstract phrases of the law."

Over the past few decades, the Supreme Court has ignored Frankfurter's warning and scampered into the political thicket. *Bush v. Gore*[2] is only the most recent, and perhaps the most extreme, foray. Other illustrations abound, some successful, others downright disastrous. In one of the proudest moments in Supreme Court history, the Court revolutionized the American political landscape by adopting the one person, one vote standard out of whole cloth, engrafting onto the Constitution's Equal Protection Clause a requirement that every vote in a legislative election be calibrated with mathematical precision to be as valuable as the next.[3] Armed with this jurisprudence, a very different Court, in a very different decade, then began second-guessing legislative judgments on how district lines ought to be drawn, ruling that race—or more specifically the intention to give communities of color a better opportunity to elect candidates of their choice—could not be the "predominant motive" (whatever that means) in the drawing of district lines.[4] Meanwhile, the Court found in the First Amendment an entirely new jurisprudence for access to the ballot, tolerating certain state-imposed barriers, but not others.[5] In one fell swoop, the Court abolished low-level patronage appointments drastically altering the way local party machines had operated for generations.[6] And, for better or worse, the Court has insinuated

---

[2]121 S. Ct. 525 (2000).

[3]*Baker v. Carr*, 369 U.S. 186 (1962) (equal protection challenges to apportionment schemes are justiciable); *Wesberry v. Sanders*, 376 U.S. 1 (1964) (Article I, section 2 of the Constitution requires that congressional districts must be apportioned on the basis of equal population); *Reynolds v. Sims*, 377 U.S. 533 (1964) (under the Equal Protection Clause, state legislative seats must be reapportioned on the basis of population); *Mahan v. Howell*, 410 U.S. 315 (1973) (some deviation from the principle of equal population is permitted in state legislative districting); *Karcher v. Daggett*, 462 U.S. 725 (1983) (the principle of equal population for congressional districts tolerates virtually no deviation).

[4]*Hunt v. Cromartie*, 526 U.S. 541 (1999); *see also Shaw v. Reno*, 509 U.S. 630 (1993); *Shaw v. Hunt*, 517 U.S. 899 (1996).

[5]*See, e.g., Williams v. Rhodes*, 393 U.S. 23 (1968) (striking requirement that candidates gather signatures equal in number to 15 percent of the vote in the previous gubernatorial election); *Jenness v. Fortson*, 403 U.S. 431 (1971) (upholding five percent requirement); *Storer v. Brown*, 415 U.S. 724 (1974) (upholding "sore loser" provision and provision prohibiting voters who participated in primaries from signing nominating petitions); *Anderson v. Celebrezze*, 460 U.S. 780 (1983) (striking early filing deadline for independent presidential candidates); *Bullock v. Carter*, 405 U.S. 134 (1972) (striking the requirement that a candidate pay a filing fee in order to get on the ballot); *Timmons v. Twin Cities Area New Party*, 520 U.S. 351 (1997) (upholding state's prohibition against "fusion" candidacies).

[6]*Rutan v. Republican Party of Illinois*, 497 U.S. 62 (1990) (banning patronage in transfer or promotion of public employees); *Elrod v. Burns*, 427 U.S. 347 (1976) (ban-

itself into legislative judgments on how political parties can organize themselves.[7]

And, of course, of greatest relevance to this volume, the Supreme Court, with some assistance from the lower courts, constructed a new, increasingly complicated, and, at times, utterly counterintuitive jurisprudence on campaign finance. Consider some of these judicial missteps: First, in its *Buckley v. Valeo*[8] decision, the Supreme Court, with Solomonic ingenuity, decided to distinguish between two types of financial transactions directed at elections—spending, which can never be limited, and contributions, which can. Some lower courts, grossly misinterpreting a footnote in that case, have decided that an advertisement is not election-related, and therefore immune from regulation, unless it includes certain "magic words" such as "vote for," "vote against," "elect," or "defeat"—words that even candidates themselves rarely use in their own electioneering messages.[9] In another line of cases, the Supreme Court, citing the need to insulate politics from large accretions of power, concluded that it is permissible to bar corporations from spending even a single penny to influence voters in candidate elections,[10] but it is not permissible to bar them from spending unlimited funds to influence voters in ballot initiatives.[11] Most recently, the Supreme Court, articulating a constitutional rule about party spending, conjured up a mutant political animal that no political scientist would ever have imagined: the political party that operates independently of its candidates.[12]

---

ning patronage firing); *see also Board of County Commissioners v. Umbehr*, 518 U.S. 668 (1996) (applying the same principle to prohibit patronage in awarding of contracts).

[7]*E.g., California Democratic Party v. Jones*, 120 S. Ct. 2402 (2000) (declaring the "blanket" primary unconstitutional); *Democratic Party of the United States v. Wisconsin*, 450 U.S. 107 (1981) (a state that requires an open primary may not require a political party to abide by the primary's results); *Eu v. San Francisco County Democratic Central Committee*, 489 U.S. 214 (1989) (striking state law prohibiting political parties from endorsing primary candidates).

[8]424 U.S. 1 (1976) *(per curiam)*.

[9]*See, e.g., FEC v. Christian Action Network, Inc.*, 110 F.3d 1049 (4th Cir. 1997) (sanctioning the FEC for taking the opposite position); *Maine Right to Life Committee, Inc. v. FEC*, 98 F.3d 1 (1996), *cert. denied*, 522 U.S. 810 (1997). *But see FEC v. Furgatch*, 807 F.2d 857 (9th Cir. 1987) (upholding an FEC regulation that departs from "magic words").

[10]*Austin v. Michigan Chamber of Commerce*, 494 U.S. 652 (1990).

[11]*First National Bank of Boston v. Bellotti*, 435 U.S. 765 (1978).

[12]*Colorado Republican Federal Campaign Committee v. FEC*, 518 U.S. 604 (1996). The political science community is in long-standing agreement that parties and candidates are institutionally and functionally intertwined. *See, e.g.,* V. O. Key, Jr., *Politics, Parties, and Pressure Groups* (5th ed., 1964); John Aldrich, *Why Parties? The Origin and Transformation of Political Parties in America* (1995). Tellingly, the only brief submitted to the *Colorado Republican* Court by political scientists adhered to this tradition,

All this, believe it or not, the Supreme Court, and lower courts, drew out of 10 words of the First Amendment, "Congress shall pass no law restricting the freedom of speech." You can almost hear old Felix chuckling, "Told you so."

It must be tempting for political scientists to feel superior. They would never have been so obtuse about political institutions. But, in all fairness to the courts, it's not as if political scientists have been such a big help. They have not been flooding the courts with useful data on which to base decisions and have rarely weighed in collectively and systematically with input on how to think about the likely impact of constitutional rulings. Political scientists could do more to explore the empirical questions on which the courts will ultimately base their legal conclusions, and so much more to communicate those facts to the courts in simple, direct terms.

This chapter offers some preliminary thoughts on areas political scientists could explore if they wish to have more of an influence on judicial decisions. I begin with a review of the current legal framework of campaign finance doctrine, set by *Buckley*, and then turn to some of *Buckley*'s basic premises that have never been subjected to rigorous assessment by the political science community. I then summarize some of the current legal controversies—from the regulation of sham issue advocacy to soft money to contribution limits to public financing—describing some of the key legal issues and the empirical questions that could help the courts resolve them. Throughout, my hope is to encourage political science research into campaign finance questions that are sure to confound the courts, so that political scientists will secure their rightful place as active participants in the formulation of constitutional principles, rather than relegating themselves to the role of mystified and incensed reporters of botched judicial forays into the political thicket.

The *Buckley* Framework

The discussion on campaign finance reform and the Constitution begins, and often ends, with *Buckley v. Valeo*, the Supreme Court's 1976 opinion that dominates the field. I'm not going to present a full critical analysis of *Buckley;* I've done that elsewhere.[13] In the interest of full disclosure, though, I will confess that I consider *Buckley* one of the most misguided opinions of the century and one that is damaging our democracy.

In *Buckley,* the Supreme Court reviewed the 1974 post-Watergate amendments to the Federal Election Campaign Act. As passed by Congress, FECA was

---

never suggesting the animal the Court hypothesized. *See* Brief for Committee on Party Renewal, *Colorado Republican, supra.*

[13]E. Joshua Rosenkranz, Buckley *Stops Here* (20th Century Fund 1998); *see also If* Buckley *Fell,* ed. E. Joshua Rosenkranz (Century Foundation 1999).

an intricate web of four integrated components. First, Congress imposed contribution caps—limits on how much a variety of political actors could put directly into each other's pockets. Most notably, FECA included limits on how much an individual could contribute to a candidate ($1,000 per election). But it also limited how much an individual could contribute to a political action committee ($5,000 per year) or a political party ($20,000 per year). It included restrictions on how much a PAC could contribute to a candidate ($5,000 per election). And it included a complicated set of limits on how much a political party could contribute directly to a candidate or spend in coordination with him.

Second, FECA established a series of mandatory spending limits—caps on how much a variety of political players could spend on advocacy in support of or against candidates for political office. FECA imposed three distinct spending limits. It limited: (1) the amount a candidate could spend of his own personal wealth (ranging from $25,000 for most House races up to $50,00 for presidential races); (2) the amount a campaign could spend from funds raised in discrete amounts ($70,000 per election for a House seat, for example); and (3) the amount an individual or group could spend independently in support of a candidate (a paltry $1,000 per election).

Third, for presidential elections, FECA established public financing conditioned on voluntary spending limits. For the primary elections, FECA provided matching funds for qualifying candidates, but only for those candidates who were prepared to abide by a complicated litany of state-by-state spending limits. For the general elections, FECA provided a large grant to each of the major party candidates—an amount that reached over $67 million per candidate in the 2000 elections—in return for their pledge not to raise any private money toward their elections.

Finally, FECA imposed stringent disclosure and reporting requirements on all the types of transactions described above. For the first time, the disclosure rules shed light on all but the most minimal contributions and expenditures directed at influencing federal elections.

Buckley is most well known for striking mandatory spending limits of all three varieties—limits on candidates, limits on campaigns, and limits on independent spending. But it is just as important to understand that the Court upheld each of the other components of the integrated regulatory scheme. The Court upheld contribution limits of all sorts and has continued to do so since.[14] The Court upheld the public financing system, including (as a later case made clear) the use of public funds to entice politicians to accept spending limits that could

---

[14]*See, e.g., California Medical Association v. FEC*, 453 U.S. 182 (1981) (upholding $5,000 limit on contributions to PACs); *Nixon v. Shrink Missouri Government PAC*, 528 U.S. 377 (2000) (upholding state contribution limits ranging from $250 to $1,075).

not be imposed on them involuntarily.[15] And the Court upheld disclosure rules, in sweeping terms, as necessary to inform voters fully about the nature of a candidate's support.

How in the world could the Supreme Court have upheld contribution limits, but declared that spending limits are never permissible? In order to understand how *Buckley* got there, and the implications for later reforms, it is important to understand three components of *Buckley*. First, contrary to popular perception, the Court never said "money equals speech." Rather, it observed that money is the fuel for speech, and, as such, limits on spending or giving money call into play First Amendment concerns. That is not to say that the First Amendment always trumps a campaign finance regulation, but rather that a court must carefully scrutinize any measure to ensure that it does not infringe unduly on speech. That much is unexceptionable. After all, a speaker could not even leaflet without buying a ream of paper. Where *Buckley* went wrong was in holding that every dollar spent on speech is as protected as the spoken word itself, but we'll get to that momentarily.

Second, *Buckley* held that contributions and expenditures must be treated differently under the First Amendment. As it does in so many areas of constitutional doctrine, the Court in this context balanced the importance of the speech right against the weightiness of the government's reasons for infringing on speech. In striking the balance, the Court concluded that spending has greater First Amendment value than contributions and that the government has a more powerful reason to limit contributions than spending.

As to the speech value of these two activities: A contribution, the Court held, has little speech value. It is a mere "signal" of support whose content and intensity do not depend very much on the size of the contribution. In the Court's (somewhat counterintuitive) estimation, a contribution communicates the same message whether it is $100 or $100,000. Spending, on the other hand, has greater speech value. It is much more akin to direct speech, because every dollar spent will actually increase the "the number of issues discussed, the depth of their exploration, and the size of the audience reached." Or so the Court thought.

As to the reasons for regulating: The Court concluded that contributions corrupt more than spending. The Court easily saw that a candidate could be corrupted by large contributions. A large campaign check could engender a political debt that a politician might feel obliged to repay with political favors in the form of official action or inaction. Or, at the very least, the Court understood that large contributions would give rise to an "appearance of corruption," which is, according to the Court, every bit as deleterious to our democracy as actual corruption. In contrast, the Court could not see how a candidate could be corrupted by unlimited spending. The Court rejected the notion that a candidate might give

---

[15]*See Republican Nat'l Comm. v. FEC,* 487 F. Supp. 280, 286 (S.D.N.Y.) (three-judge court).

special consideration to a supporter who independently spends $1 million on television ads supporting his election rather than writing a much smaller check directly to the campaign. Nor did the Court recognize any danger that the endless money chase might corrupt a candidate's agenda or priorities.

Third, *Buckley* held that corruption is the only rationale that will justify any restrictions on campaign finance (or, more accurately, that it was the only legitimate rationale among those presented in defense of FECA). Specifically, the Court rejected any notion that the government might limit the flow of money into elections in the name of equality. The Court famously opined, "the concept that government may restrict the speech of some elements of our society in order to enhance the relative voice of others is wholly foreign to the First Amendment." In essence, *Buckley* said that government couldn't impose reasonable rules of the game. We cannot impose Robert's Rules of Order on elections as we do for just about every other area of public life where we engage in debate directed at educating an audience.

The upshot of the Court's analysis is that spending limits of any sort are unconstitutional—unless they are imposed as a condition of the receipt of public funds, so that candidates remain free to reject them. But contribution limits are constitutional, so long as they are not set too low. How low is too low? The Court back then shed no light on this question, except to say that a contribution limit is too low when it becomes "a difference in kind" rather than "a difference in degree"—whatever that means.

A generation later, *Buckley*'s basic construct remains the law. But the edifice is cracking. Six out of nine justices have expressed doubts as to *Buckley*'s most vulnerable premise—that spending limits and contributions limits should be treated differently under the First Amendment.[16] The catch is that they are split as to which way this rotting tree should fall. Should both kinds of limits be permissible, or neither? Justices Scalia and Thomas are flatly on record as saying that the Constitution commands complete deregulation, and Justice Kennedy has indicated a tentative attraction to that proposition, while acknowledging that he is open to persuasion on the opposite conclusion. Justices Ginsburg and Stevens are on record, as saying they think both should be regulated, with Justice Breyer adding a very clear signal that he is on board with them. Justice Souter, Justice O'Connor, and Chief Justice Rehnquist (who signed onto the distinction in the original *Buckley* Court) have not tipped their hands.

It seems inevitable that *Buckley* will fall. Whether it does, and which way, could depend on the extent to which the real experts lend their assistance to the Supreme Court in a succession of cases that is likely to culminate in the ultimate challenge to *Buckley*.

---

[16]See *Shrink Missouri, supra.*

Buckley's Unexplored Premises

Courts move slowly. That proposition, as frustrating as it may be to us liti-gators and self-appointed law reformers, should be good news to scholars who might aspire to influence the way the Supreme Court thinks about campaign finance. Even though most of the justices have already abandoned *Buckley*'s core analysis, the ultimate challenge to *Buckley* is probably several years away. That gives the political science community plenty of time to scrutinize and ex-plore some of the assumptions at the heart of the case—assumptions about the impact of spending limits on speech, about the corrupting nature of spending, about the impact of contribution limits, and about a host of possible alternative justifications for spending limits.

Impact on Speech

Recall that a main reason the *Buckley* Court struck spending limits was its sense that the amount of money spent on a campaign correlated with "the num-ber of issues discussed, the depth of their exploration, and the size of the audi-ence reached." The Court was probably right—to an extent—about the size of the audience reached. Surely, each repetition of a campaign ad will catch the attention of *some* voter who had not yet seen it. But the courts have had little guidance to assess the marginal impact of each additional dollar on the number of voters reached with a message. More to the point, though, the courts have no basis on which to evaluate the more important part of the premise—that each additional increment of campaign spending necessarily expands the number of issues explored and the depth of their exploration. To what extent does spending translate into more campaign issues or deeper and longer conversation about them? My hunch is that the meteoric rise in sending over the past two decades has coincided with a dumbing down and shortening of political messages. In-deed, I would think, it's probably the candidates with the *least* money who have no choice but to participate in debates, which are far more informative than your typical TV spots. But concrete data are sparse.

What about past history? Are there measurable differences in the content of discourse before FECA, when spending in presidential elections was uncapped, and in the few cycles after FECA, when every major-party candidate voluntarily capped spending in return for public financing? Have the number of issues and depth of coverage shot up over the past few election cycles as more and more money has poured into elections through the soft money loophole? Studies that evaluate these sorts of questions are sure to influence whether the Supreme Court ultimately adheres to this premise.

Quid Pro Quo Corruption

Political scientists have spilt quite a bit of ink over how much campaign contributions influence the behavior of officeholders.[17] But they have devoted less attention to the impact of independent spending on officeholders' behavior. *Buckley*'s premise was that contributors are more likely to corrupt than independent spenders because spending might not necessarily help a candidate, and there is no direct transaction between the spender and the candidate. The Court was so confident of this assessment that it was willing to allow a ban on contributions larger than $1,000 while prohibiting any cap on spending, even in the range of $1 million, $10 million, or more.

There is plenty of room for exploration of whether this proposition is demonstrably true—or false. Are candidates any more likely to provide access to those who have supported them with large independent expenditures? What was the real effect of independent spending and issue ads on elections? How often are they actually detrimental to a candidate they are designed to promote, as the Supreme Court posited?

In a related vein, the Supreme Court saw absolutely no benefit in limiting a candidate's fundraising, once contribution limits are in place. As the Court saw it, if a $1,000 contribution is not corrupting, then what could possibly be the harm of allowing a candidate to raise a thousand or 10,000 contributions of that size? What the Court ignored is that contributions are not infinitely fungible. Any candidate will acknowledge that some contributions are harder to raise than others. That is but a small step from saying that a candidate risks compromising himself more for some donations than others. That is a possible argument for capping fundraising. But there is little data with which to assess the argument. Is there any way to assess whether some contributions are more corrupting than others? Would a candidate be more likely to decline contributions from certain

---

[17]Most of the political science literature recognizes that campaign contributions tend to purchase "access" to officeholders. *See, e.g.,* John C. Green, Paul S. Herrnson, Lynda Powell, Clyde Wilcox, *Individual Congressional Campaign Contributors: Wealthy, Conservative, and Reform-Minded* (Joyce Foundation 1998). But, political science research is divided on whether "access" translates into "influence" over officeholders. Many political scientists believe that campaign contributions are a means to influence legislation and public policies. *See, e.g.,* Frank Sorauf, *Inside Campaign Finance* (1992); Richard L. Hall & Frank W. Wayman, "Buying Time: Moneyed Interests and the Mobilization of Bias in Congressional Committees," 84 *Am. Pol. Sci. Rev.* 797 (1990); Anne Bedlington, "Loopholes & Abuses," in *Money, Elections & Democracy* (Margaret Nuget and John Johannes, eds., 1990), 69; Kenneth Levit, "Campaign Finance Reform & the Returns of Buckley v. Valeo," 103 *Yale L. J.* 469, 473 (1993). But many others argue that "access" does not usually translate into "influence." *See* John Wright, *Interest Groups and Congress: Lobbying, Contributions, and Influence* (Allyn & Bacon 1996), 136–149 (reviewing literature).

sources more than others if spending limits capped the sheer number of contributions he was in a position to accept?

Preserving Candidates' Time

Forget about corruption for a moment. Any reconsideration of *Buckley* will almost certainly entail an examination of alternative rationales for spending limits. One of the leading alternatives is that spending limits are necessary to discipline incumbents to tend to the business of governing. The argument is that fundraising has become an enormous distraction and that limiting fundraising is as justifiable as prohibiting officeholders from moonlighting in another job. But the argument is rooted in little more than anecdote.[18] A systematic study of how much time candidates actually spend raising money would be very valuable, as would an analysis of whether candidates spend more time with those who have or can make contributions than with other constituents. Conversely, it would be worth noting whether self-financing incumbents or those in safe seats spend more time on government business or meeting with the voting constituency than candidates who are stuck in the money chase.

The other side of this issue is also worthy of exploration. Those who oppose limits on fundraising insist that it is a healthy brand of constituent contact. A candidate forced to raise funds has to spend time with constituents and is more likely to feel accountable to them. It is worth exploring how modern day fundraising compares to other sorts of constituency contact. Do candidates learn as much about their constituents' needs by dialing for dollars as they do, for example, by attending barbecues or shaking hands in malls? What do candidates themselves say about this? Given their druthers, which would they rather do? Which do they think is a better way of staying attuned to their constituents?

Enhancing Competition

Advocates on both sides of the legal debate cite the promise of enhanced competition as a leading reason to revisit *Buckley*. Those who would strike contribution limits argue that contribution limits protect incumbents. Incumbents have the rolodexes and the fundraising apparatuses to raise mountains of checks quickly, whereas challengers must start from scratch. If only contribution limits were lifted, the argument goes, challengers would become competitive simply

---

[18]*See* Martin Schram, *Speaking Freely* (Center for Responsive Politics 1995); Phillip Stern, *Still the Best Congress Money Can Buy* (Regnery 1992). An exception is a recent study by Paul Herrnson, which is not yet published.

by raising a few large checks from ardent supporters, as Eugene McCarthy did when he launched his insurgent presidential campaign.

The rebuttal is that incumbents will always outstrip challengers in extracting contributions—of any size—from donors. If we lift contribution limits, incumbents, too, will be permitted to raise enormous contributions, and they will have more clout with which to extract them. Challengers will still be at a competitive disadvantage; only the numbers—and the minimum price tag needed to be competitive—will skyrocket. Adherents to this view are more likely to view spending limits as the best way to increase competition. They argue that the biggest barrier to entry into politics is the sheer amount of money a candidate has to raise in order to be considered viable. That barrier seems higher when a would-be challenger knows that his opponent could outspend him many, many times over.

Much good work has been done of late to explore the extent to which spending levels influence election outcomes.[19] More research along the lines suggested above could be very informative on this fundamental policy question. Those who would consider abandoning contribution limits need to have a better sense of who would benefit from such a step. Would challengers in fact be empowered by a handful of generous contributions that launch their campaigns, or would that edge be completely overwhelmed by the ability of incumbents to extract many more large gifts from people with business before them?

---

[19]The political science literature divides into three competing schools on the impact of campaign spending on electoral outcomes, although all agree that campaign spending has a decisive impact on elections. One school argues that campaign spending by challengers has a greater influence on election outcomes than spending by incumbents. *See* Gary Jacobson, "The Effects of Campaign Spending on Congressional Elections," 72 *Amer. Pol. Sci. Rev.* 469–491(1978); Gary Jacobson, *Money in Congressional Elections* (1980); Gary Jacobson, "The Effects of Campaign Spending in House Elections," 34 *Amer. J. of Pol. Sci.* 334–62 (1990). A second school insists that spending by both challengers and incumbents has a significant, and nearly identical, effect on election outcomes. *See* Donald Green and Jonathan Krasno, "Rebuttal to Jacobson's 'New Evidence for Old Arguments,'" 34 *Amer. J. of Pol. Sci.* 363–72 (1990); Christopher Kenny and Michael McBurnett, "An Individual Level Multiequation Model of Expenditure Effects in Contested House Elections," 88 *Amer. Pol. Sci. Rev.* 699–707 (1994); A. Gerber, "Estimating the Effects of Campaign Spending on Senate Election Outcomes Using Instrumental Variables," 92 *Amer. Pol. Sci. Rev.* 401–11 (1998); Randall Partin, "Revisiting Campaign Spending in Governor's Races" (1999) (presented at the 1999 annual meeting of the Western Political Science Association). Still, a third school, which does not necessarily contradict either of the first two, argues that the effectiveness of campaign spending follows a bell-curve—that is, spending is very effective at influencing elections up to a point, and then declines in effectiveness as spending becomes excessive and redundant. *See* Gary Copeland, "The Impact of Money on Congressional Elections" (2000) (presented at the 2000 annual meeting of the American Political Science Association).

And what of the factors that contribute to a challenger's decision whether to run for office? There has been some good research on what attributes make a challenger strong.[20] But equally important is what factors make a challenger run—or decline to run? To what extent does the fundraising arms race repel challengers? If candidates had to raise less money in order to be effective, would more, or better, candidates emerge?

Sham Issue Advocacy

We have been focusing on questions that are relevant to a distant legal controversy involving a reconsideration of principles pronounced 25 years ago. But some of the most significant legal issues in campaign finance regulation are much more current and imminent. And those issues, too, cry out for serious consideration by, and input from, the political science community. Perhaps the thorniest legal issue in the field of campaign finance regulation involves constitutional constraints on the regulation of money directed toward sham issue advocacy—ads that look, smell, waddle, and quack like campaign ads, but escape regulation because the sponsor pretends to be engaged in advocacy on issues.

Buckley and later cases have made this much clear: Elections are so special that it is permissible to draw a line around election-related speech and regulate it in ways that are not permissible with regard to other political speech. When it comes to electioneering, we can limit the source of funds (including an outright prohibition on corporate and union funds), we can limit fundraising, and we can require disclosure of amounts raised and spent. The question is exactly where a legislature may draw the line. In other words, what are the constraints on a legislature's power to define what is considered "electioneering," and therefore subject to special restrictions. The Supreme Court grappled with this issue very cursorily in Buckley—leaving the lower courts confused ever since. FECA, the 1974 act discussed earlier, had several provisions purporting to define the speech that was subject to its regulation. FECA's spending limits applied to any spending "relative to a clearly identified candidate in federal elections." FECA's disclosure rules applied to anyone "who makes contributions or expenditures . . . for the purpose of . . . influencing the nomination or election of candidates for federal office." The Court found both these provisions unconstitutionally vague. The average speaker couldn't possibly know whether some fact finder would later declare his words to have been "relative to" a candidate or "for the purpose

---

[20]Gary Jacobson and S. Kernell, Strategy and Choice in Congressional Elections (Yale 1981); Donald Green and Jonathan Krasno, "Salvation for the Spendthrift Incumbent: Reestimating the Effects of Campaign Spending in House Elections," 34 Amer. Pol. Sci. Rev. 363–72 (1988); Paul Herrnson, "Campaign Professionalism and Fundraising in Congressional Elections," 54 J. Pol. 859–70 (1992).

of . . . influencing" an election. Vagueness of that sort raises problems, especially in the context of regulating speech, for it leaves the speaker to censor himself out of fear that he might accidentally trip across the line. Courts call this, somewhat ominously, the "chilling effect."

Having found that Congress had not done a sufficiently good job of defining the line distinguishing electioneering from other political speech, the Court could have struck the entire regulatory regime as unconstitutional. Instead, the Court did Congress's job for it. In order to save the rest of the statute, the Court engrafted onto the law a very restrictive definition of electioneering. The Court decided to read FECA to cover only "communications that expressly advocate the election or defeat of a clearly identified candidate." In a now-famous footnote, the Court expanded upon its definition, explaining that "express advocacy" meant explicit words "of advocacy of election or defeat, such as 'vote for,' 'elect,' 'support,' 'cast your ballot for,' 'Smith for Congress,' 'vote against,' 'defeat,' [or] 'reject.'"

By virtue of the Supreme Court's intervention, any advertisement that avoids these "magic words" or others like them escapes regulation under FECA. As a consequence, corporations, labor unions, and wealthy individuals have in recent years gotten away with pumping enormous sums into federal elections, in amounts far exceeding the permissible limits. They have done so without revealing to the public the sources of the funds or the magnitude of the spending.

This enormous loophole has led members of Congress—and legislators or initiative drafters in the states—to develop alternative definitions of electioneering. The question before the courts, a question that will ultimately reach the Supreme Court soon, is how to evaluate such redefinitions. Most courts have declared, somewhat myopically, that the Supreme Court in *Buckley* announced the only permissible standard, and that any departure from the magic words test is unconstitutional.[21] Others have suggested that other sensitively drawn lines may

---

[21] *See Iowa Right to Life Comm., Inc. v. Williams,* 187 F.3d 963 (8th Cir. 1999) (granting preliminary injunction against definition of "express advocacy" in state law that went beyond magic words); *FEC v. Christian Action Network, Inc.,* 110 F.3d 1049, 1061–62 (4th Cir. 1997) (invalidating federal regulation defining express advocacy to include more than magic words); *Maine Right to Life Comm., Inc. v. FEC,* 98 F.3d 1 (1st Cir. 1996) (*per curiam*) (same); *Vermont Right to Life Comm., Inc. v. Sorrell,* 221 F.3d 376, 389 (2d Cir. 2000) (striking a provision requiring reporting of expenditures of $500 or more for mass media activities including the name or likeness of a candidate and run within 30 days of an election); *Planned Parenthood Affiliates of Michigan, Inc. v. Miller,* 21 F. Supp. 2d 740, 746 (E.D. Mich. 1998) (striking provision that barred corporations and unions from paying for communications containing the name or likeness of a candidate within 45 days of an election); *Right to Life of Michigan, Inc. v. Miller,* 23 F. Supp. 2d 766, 771 (W.D. Mich. 1998) (same).

be permissible.[22]

The basic parameters by which the Court will resolve the issue are clear. Any attempt at drawing the line must navigate between a Scylla and Charybdis of constitutional doctrines. On the one hand, the definition must be sufficiently precise to allow a putative speaker to know with reasonable certainty whether the words he is about to utter will bring him within the ambit of regulation. (That's where FECA's definitions went astray.) On the other hand, even the clearest statute must not be "overbroad"; the drafter must tailor the provision narrowly so that it doesn't accidentally sweep within its ambit too much speech that is unrelated to elections (and therefore lacking the special characteristics that justify regulation). Think of this as like trying to catch tuna without catching too many dolphins.

There are two leading models that have been batted around as possible alternatives to the magic words test. The first model entails some variation of the "reasonable person" test common in so many other areas of the law. It might declare an ad to be electioneering if a reasonable person viewing the ad would believe it to have an electioneering purpose. Or, on the far more protective end of the spectrum, an ad might be deemed electioneering only if no reasonable person could conclude its purpose is anything other than to influence an election. A second model is the bright-line test. Typically, it identifies an ad as electioneering if it mentions a clearly identified candidate and runs within a fixed time period (typically 30 or 60 days) before the election.

The first model has fallen under attack as too vague. Who knows, the argument goes, what a hypothetical reasonable person would say? The second has fallen under attack as too broad, sweeping within its regulatory ambit speech honestly not intended to influence an election. The hypothetical example always trotted out is an ad within 30 days of a presidential election urging the incumbent president to take some important action (for example, to stop bombing Cambodia, or to settle an airline strike).

For the past few years, courts, legislatures, and advocates grappling with these provisions have made sweeping claims about the nature of political speech, the types of people who run political ads, or the average speaker's ability to distinguish between electioneering messages and educational messages. Opponents would paint a picture of scores of activists in the final weeks of a Congress taking out ads to try to influence their representatives' votes on critical legislative matters, only to learn that they had run afoul of campaign finance

---

[22]See *FEC v. Furgatch*, 807 F.2d 857, 864 (9th Cir. 1987) (finding express advocacy even without magic words); *Elections Board of Wisconsin v. Wisconsin Manufacturers and Commerce*, 597 N.W.2d 721, 730–31 (Wis.), *cert. denied*, 120 S. Ct. 408 (1999) (rejecting the idea that express advocacy requires use of magic words); *State ex rel. Crumpton v. Keisling*, 982 P.2d 3, 10–11 (Ore. App. 1999), *review denied*, 994 P.2d 132 (Ore. 2000).

laws. Or they would conjure up little old ladies who pool their money to buy an ad urging the president to sign a prescription drug benefit, only to face prosecution. Or a gay soldier who wants to support a media campaign urging a member of Congress to vote for hate crimes legislation, only to learn his identity will be revealed and his career ruined.

All those claims were rooted in nothing but anecdote, hypothesis, and speculation. No one had gathered serious data with which to answer some of the critical questions at the heart of the most important campaign finance debate of the decade. What are the usual attributes of election-related speech? How hard is it to distinguish between electioneering and other political speech? Can average observers distinguish the two with reasonable certainty and near unanimity? How often do ads appear close to the election, identifying a candidate, but not intending to influence the election? Who tends to sponsor these ads?

Recent empirical efforts have targeted these questions. For example, the Brennan Center for Justice, in partnership with Professor Kenneth Goldstein of the University of Wisconsin-Madison, has developed a database that includes every political advertisement run in the 1998 and the 2000 federal elections in the largest 75 media markets (encompassing 80 percent of the U.S. population) and the 25 largest cable networks.[23] We are still working through the 2000 data, but from the 1998 data we made several discoveries. We learned, for example, that 96 percent of all ads run by candidates—ads that were unquestionably electioneering—did not use any magic words. So much for the notion that magic words could be the touchstone for what constitutes electioneering. We also discovered that coders had little trouble determining with certainty the purpose of a particular ad even when it did not use magic words. We found that more than 90 percent of all sham issue ads are run by political parties, major national advocacy organizations, or business groups—all of whom are likely to have counsel advising them every step of the way—not little old ladies. And, most importantly, we found that overbreadth concerns regarding a bright-line test were overblown: Among the thousands of unique ads we collected, two were sponsored by independent groups, named a candidate, and ran within 60 days of an election, but were intended to be educational rather than electioneering.

But this was just a beginning. Our database, which is available to the entire political science community, could occupy a team of political scientists with worthwhile projects for years to come. And there is a lot more data to collect and questions to answer before we can feel satisfied that political science has given meaningful input into this thorny set of questions.

---

[23]Jonathan S. Krasno and Daniel Seltz, *Buying Time* (Brennan Center for Justice 2000); *see also* David B. Magleby, *Dictum without Data* (Center for the Study of Elections & Democracy 2000) (demonstrating that the "magic words" test does not distinguish electioneering from issue advocacy).

Soft Money

The most high-profile debate on campaign finance these days is about soft money, which presents a variation on the sham issue advocacy themes. Soft money is the name for the enormous contributions that political parties raise from corporations, unions, and wealthy individuals. As we have seen, candidates are prohibited from raising large contributions—or from raising any money at all from corporations or labor unions. And corporations and labor unions are prohibited from giving or spending money to influence elections. Soft money is an end run around these prohibitions. The political parties enlist candidates to raise money in large sums from corporations, unions, and wealthy individuals and funnel that money into ads that benefit those very same candidates, typically by targeting their opponents. These ads are identical to candidate ads. Only they scrupulously avoid any magic words, allowing the party to claim they didn't use the money from these prohibited sources for electioneering, but rather for general education on issues.

It seems certain that Congress will pass a soft money ban soon. It seems just as certain that the ban will be challenged. Indeed, the Republican National Committee has already filed a challenge to the current restrictions on soft money—marginally inconvenient allocation formulas requiring political parties to mix a certain amount of hard money (regulated money raised in smaller amounts from individuals and PACs under FECA's rules) into their soft money spending, on the ground that the spending of soft money inevitably has some effect on elections.

The RNC suit notwithstanding, the soft money question is a no-brainer. For this entire century it has been clear that Congress can preclude corporations (and later, unions) from giving money to candidates or to political parties. And for a generation, it has been clear that Congress can limit the size of contributions by very wealthy players to candidates or to parties. Plus, the Supreme Court has made clear that a legislature can impose regulations designed to ensure that valid restrictions are not evaded. These rules converge to mean that a ban on soft money—which is nothing more than a limit on the amount that any individual could give to a political party and a bar on corporate or labor contributions—would be upheld.

Nevertheless, the challenge will undoubtedly proceed. At its heart will be a claim that political parties need soft money in order to play the very important role they must play in our democracy. This is a proposition on which the courts could certainly use some scholarly input. It is an article of faith among political scientists that strong parties are good for our democracy. But the political science community seems to have conducted little scholarly discussion on whether soft money actually strengthens political parties in meaningful ways—i.e., in ways that enhance their salutary role in our democracy. Does soft money, raised largely by legislative committees, increase party cohesion? Does it enhance party discipline? Does it significantly increase a party's ability, and willingness, to field and promote challengers? While these questions may not ultimately be at the heart of any judicial ruling on the validity of a soft money ban, the courts could certainly benefit from political science input into each of these issues.

Low Contribution Limits

One area that has gotten a bit of judicial attention of late has been the evaluation of lower contribution limits. Recall that the Supreme Court upheld contribution limits in principle, so long as they do not dip too low. Taking advantage of this latitude, reformers over the past decade had taken to ratcheting down contribution limits across the nation, sometimes passing limits as low as $100 or even $50. That practice raised the question, how low is too low?

In *Buckley*, the Supreme Court declared that it would defer to legislative judgments. But the courts had been second-guessing the judgments of legislatures and initiatives, increasingly striking not just the $100 contribution limits that were in vogue for a time, but limits that depart from the $1,000 limits sustained by *Buckley*.[24] Then came a case out of Missouri that put the very existence of contribution limits in doubt. A federal appellate court ruled that Missouri's limits—$1,075 for statewide races—were unconstitutionally low.[25] The argument was that $1,000 in the days of *Buckley* was worth only about a third that amount today, and besides a state legislature must affirmatively establish

---

[24]*See Russell v. Burris*, 146 F.3d 563, 573 (8th Cir. 1998) (invalidating Arkansas's $100 and $300 limits on contributions to legislative and statewide candidates), *cert. denied*, 525 U.S. 1001 (1998) *and* 525 U.S. 1145 (1999); *Carver v. Nixon*, 72 F.3d 633, 645 (8th Cir. 1995) (invalidating Missouri's $100 and $300 limits on contributions to legislative and statewide candidates); *Citizens for Responsible Gov't State Political Action Comm. v. Buckley*, 60 F. Supp. 2d 1066, 1099 (D. Colo. 1999) (invalidating Colorado's $100 and $500 limits on contributions to legislative and statewide candidates); *California ProLife Council Political Action Comm. v. Scully*, 989 F. Supp. 1282, 1297 (E.D. Cal. 1998), *aff'd*, 164 F.3d 1189 (9th Cir. 1999); *National Black Police Ass'n v. District of Columbia Bd. of Elections & Ethics*, 924 F. Supp. 270, 281 (D.D.C. 1996) (invalidating Washington, D.C.'s $50 and $100 limits on contributions to city council and mayoral candidates), *vacated as moot*, 108 F.3d 346 (D.C. Cir. 1997). *But see Daggett v. Webster*, 81 F. Supp. 2d 128 (D. Me.), *aff'd sub nom. Daggett v. Commission on Gov'tal Ethics & Election Practices*, 205 F.3d 445 (1st Cir. 2000); *State v. Alaska Civil Liberties Union*, 978 P.2d 597, 634 (Alaska 1999) (upholding Alaska's $500 annual limit on contributions to all candidates), *cert. denied*, 120 S. Ct. 1156 (2000).

[25]*See Shrink Missouri Government PAC v. Adams*, 161 F.3d 519, 523 (8th Cir. 1998).

the existence of corruption in order to sustain its limits. It was a ruling that cast a shadow on federal limits and the limits of most states.

The Supreme Court, in *Nixon v. Shrink Missouri Government PAC*,[26] categorically rejected the notion that constitutional rights have to be indexed for inflation, as well as the idea that the corrupting influence of money has to be proven with every enactment. The Court then set an exceedingly low threshold for judicial approval of contribution limits. Contribution limits would be upheld, the Court declared, unless they were "so radical in effect as to render political association ineffective, drive the sound of a candidate's voice below the level of notice, and render contributions pointless."

In the interest of full disclosure, I should mention that the Brennan Center litigated the *Shrink Missouri* case and proposed that standard for judging contribution limits. It was one of a series of cases we litigated involving the permissible level of contribution limits. Throughout those litigations, we were struck by a major gap in the political science literature. Political scientists had devoted considerable energy to the issue of spending, particularly to the impact of spending levels on electoral outcomes. But they had devoted virtually no energy to assessing the impact of lowering (or raising) contribution limits. There was no political science literature, for example, describing how candidates might adapt to the lowering of contribution limits. Would they simply use different fundraising techniques, but still raise the same amounts? Those who have attacked contribution limits have typically resorted to what one court recently derided as "worst-case scenario statistics, which consider the historical funding pattern and discount any contribution made over the limit."[27] That practice, the court concluded, overpredicts the loss of contributions. In a veritable plea to political scientists, the court observed: "It is the statistics distilled from experience"—such as cross-jurisdictional studies or studies of campaign finance systems over time—"that, far more than worst-case scenarios, should inform decisions as to proper contribution limits."

Similarly, there is little literature on what amounts of money were necessary to reach voters anyway. Is it true, as so many self-interested political consultants insist, that saturating the airwaves with very expensive commercials is the only way to run a statewide race? Or is it possible to penetrate the voters' consciousness as effectively through other means?

The Supreme Court has resolved the main legal issues surrounding contribution limits—and no lower court has invalidated a contribution limit since *Shrink Missouri*[28]—but these political science questions remain important. Ju-

---

[26]528 U.S. 377 (2000).

[27]*Daggett v. Commission on Gov'tal Ethics & Election Practices*, 205 F.3d 445 (1st Cir. 2000).

[28]*See Montana Right to Life Ass'n, et al. v. Eddleman et ano*, No. CV 96–165-BLG-JDS, slip op. at 9–10 (D. Mont. Sept. 19, 2000) (upholding Montana's $100, $200, and

risdictions may still pass laws that could raise questions even under the Court's new standard. But even failing that, legislators considering where to set their contribution limits—and even whether to raise them—could benefit a great deal from fuller information on the impact of changes of this sort. Moreover, the last set of questions—about what kinds of resources are needed to reach voters— figure prominently in other legal battles that are already brewing, including the battles over full public financing.

Public Financing

The Supreme Court made it clear in *Buckley* that a legislature is allowed to en- tice candidates to cap their own expenditures voluntarily, even though it cannot require them to do it by direct command. While the courts have largely upheld these measures, some have fallen into legal pitfalls,[29] and the challenges are sure to continue. The legal questions to which political science could contribute fall into two main categories.

The first set of questions revolves around whether the spending limit is vol- untary. Can a deal be too sweet to be voluntary? Some courts have held as much, observing "there is a point at which regulatory incentives stray beyond the pale, creating disparities so profound that they become impermissibly coer- cive."[30] The deal for the presidential general elections, which the Supreme Court upheld as voluntary, has been so attractive that no major-party nominee has ever turned it down, not even George W. Bush, who did opt out of the primary sys- tem in order to remain unconstrained in his spending. That would suggest that

---

$400 limits on contributions to legislative candidates, statewide candidates other than governor and lieutenant governor, and candidates jointly filed for the offices of governor and lieutenant governor); *Daggett v. Commission on Gov'tal Ethics & Election Practices,* 205 F.3d 445, 461–62 (1st Cir. 2000) (upholding Maine's $250 limit on contributions to legislative candidates); *Shrink Missouri Gov't PAC v. Adams,* 204 F.3d 838, 840 (8th Cir. 2000) (upholding Missouri's $275, $550, and $1,075 limits on contributions to House, Senate, and statewide candidates); *Landell v. Sorrell,* 2000 WL 114080 (D. Vt. Aug. 10, 2000) (upholding Vermont's limits of $200, $300, and $400 per two-year election cycle for candidates for state House, Senate, and statewide office); *Florida Right to Life, Inc., et al. v. Mortham, et al.,* No. 6:98–770-CIV–ORL–19A, slip op. at 20–21 (M.D. Fla. Mar. 17, 2000) (upholding Florida's $500 limit "even though candidates in Florida are raising fewer funds than they are capable of raising and fewer funds than were actually raised under previous limits").

[29]*See Gable v. Patton,* 142 F.3d 940 (6th Cir. 1998), *cert. denied,* 525 U.S. 1777 (1999); *Rosenstiel v. Rodriguez,* 101 F.3d 1544 (8th Cir. 1996); *Vote Choice, Inc. v. DiStefano,* 4 F.3d 26 (1st Cir. 1993); *Republican Nat'l Comm. v. FEC,* 487 F. Supp. 280 (S.D.N.Y.) (three-judge court), *aff'd,* 445 U.S. 955 (1980).

[30]*Rosenstiel v. Rodriguez,* 101 F.3d 1544 (8th Cir. 1996).

whether or not a spending limit is voluntary should be judged on the basis of whether candidates who opt out are in some way punished, not on the basis of some judgment that the rewards of participating are too good to turn down.

Yet, the courts are increasingly facing challenges along those lines and have been known to find certain deals too sweet.[31] As these cases continue to arise, any court that is willing to entertain such a concept will almost necessarily need help from political science. How does one assess the candidates' decisions to accept or reject public financing? What factors play into those decisions? Are the factors primarily economic or political?

Also subject to challenge have been various techniques for labeling those candidates who opt in or opt out of the spending limits.[32] Over the next few years, we can expect cases to address whether those techniques—designations on the ballot or on campaign literature—amount to punishments of those who opt out. Critical to that discussion will be an understanding of how voters process the information. Is a ballot (or voter guide) designation describing the candidate as one who accepted public financing likely to skew the vote in the candidate's favor? What if the ballot (or voter guide) described the candidate as a clean candidate? Is the answer different if the candidate's name bears a star or an asterisk, which is then explained at the bottom?

The second set of questions revolves around so-called "trigger provisions," which increase the public financing available to certain candidates depending upon the conduct of others.[33] In some models, the state increases the grant to a candidate who accepts spending limits when his opponent's spending crosses a certain threshold. In other models, the public subsidy to the candidate increases when an independent group spends a considerable sum to attack him. Again, the legal question will be whether those extra grants "punish" the speech of the candidate who opts out or the speech of the independent voices. There is a very strong argument that the answer to that question is no, even if, as a factual matter, the trigger provision makes it less likely that a candidate will opt out or less likely that an independent group will spend money. After all, the argument goes,

---

[31]*See Wilkinson v. Jones,* 876 F. Supp. 916, 928 (W.D. Ky. 1995) (5–1 disparity in contribution levels, combined with 2–1 matching fund subsidy, pushed Kentucky scheme "beyond the pale").

[32]*See Daggett v. Commission on Gov'tal Ethics & Election Practices,* 74 F. Supp. 2d 53 (D. Me. 1999), *aff'd,* 205 F.3d 445 (1st Cir. 2000) (observing that any official labeling of candidates would be "most troubling," but concluding that Maine law did not affix any labels); *Colorado Right to Life Committee, Inc. v. Buckley,* No. 96–S–2844, slip op. at 10, 15-23 (D. Colo. Apr. 17, 1998) (unpublished opinion) (striking Colorado's requirement that ballots indicate which candidates have and have not accepted the voluntary spending limits).

[33]*Compare Day v. Holahan,* 34 F.3d 1356, 1362 (8th Cir. 1994) *with Daggett, supra.*

the First Amendment guarantees a speaker only the right to speak, not the right to speak without rebuttal.

On the other hand, a court assessing these provisions might well wish to know exactly what impact they have on the conduct of both candidates and independent groups. Are they less likely to spend money advertising when they know that their efforts will actually increase the resources available to the candidate they oppose? Are these provisions necessary in order to entice candidates to opt into the public financing system? At the moment, it may be impossible to answer these questions with any kind of confidence, since most of these campaign finance laws are relatively new. But as time goes on it could be very valuable for political scientists to assess their impact and their justification.

Conclusion

My goal here has been to demonstrate the wide variety of campaign-finance-related research projects on which the courts could use help. And this chapter only begins to scratch the surface. Every single one of these questions is likely to be before the courts over the next decade—some of them much earlier. There is no question that the courts will continue to venture deep into the political thicket. The only question is whether political scientists will be on hand to guide them out unscathed.

Chapter 8

Eight Modest Ideas for Meaningful Campaign Finance Reform

Norman J. Ornstein

Campaign finance reform has been a hot topic in Washington almost since the last major reform was passed in 1974 and a version implemented after the 1976 Supreme Court decision of *Buckley v. Valeo*. As campaign costs escalated in the 1980s and 1990s, and especially as the role of parties and outside groups changed in the past decade, the topic became even hotter. But high and increasing temperatures for issues do not necessarily mean action on those issues, much less policy reform enactment.

And the history of campaign finance reform over the past decade at least has been frustration, deadlock, partisan division, and inaction. The history, to be sure, has had many interesting variations, including years when versions of reform passed both houses and ended up vetoed by a president (Bush the first.), passed one house but not the other, passed the House and ended up stymied by a filibuster in the Senate, and so on. But the outcome has been the same.

Why no reform? There are many reasons. The American political system makes any enactment of a new law difficult. Reform of the political system, especially in an area that directly shapes the lives and careers of the lawmakers drafting the reform, is especially hard to implement. A majority of the lawmakers may find the existing laws unfortunate, misdirected, unpleasant, and wrongheaded. But by definition, the 535 members of Congress owe their success to the existing campaign finance laws. Changes in the status quo may jeopardize their positions, and in any event will involve major opportunity costs to those who have learned the existing rules and operate with them.

While all incumbent lawmakers are by definition successful under the existing system, the political parties have different strengths and weaknesses that make elements of the system work more or less successfully for them. So each party tends to have its own ideas for reform that are viewed with suspicion by the other party, causing a natural partisan division on the issue.

Moreover, political reform, often popular with voters, is rarely if ever high on the public's priority list. Even though surveys show a large majority of Americans have long favored campaign finance reform, they tend to rank it way below issues like education, health, Social Security, crime, the environment, or other substantive issues as a priority. A part of the reason for this lower priority is public cynicism; Americans believe that politicians will use any campaign finance system to their own advantage, that special interests will find a way to exert inordinate influence, and that lawmakers can't be trusted to write the laws that police them.

In addition, there are substantive problems. Finding a "solution" to the "problem" of campaign financing requires first defining the problem and then crafting a set of laws that will change the existing system to help solve the problem. But the problem is multifaceted, including elements like the potential or reality of corruption, the multiple "barriers for entry" for candidates caused by the high cost of campaigns, the advantages of incumbency, the large amounts of time lawmakers have to spend raising the money to run, and many more. And each proposed solution has unintended consequences that can ameliorate its impact or lead to the opposite effect from that intended. As if that weren't enough, reforming American campaign finance laws has an additional roadblock—the First Amendment and the Supreme Court's interpretation of it make any regulation of political speech, especially the crucial variety of it, campaign speech, difficult to craft.

For all these difficulties, reform is neither unachievable nor undesirable. There are clear problems in the system, and they have gotten worse over the decade of the 1990s. There are some clear incremental, constitutional steps that can be taken to rein in some of the worst elements of campaign behavior by candidates, government officials, parties, and outside groups.

Much of the rhetoric about campaign reform, and many of the proposed reforms, has been generated for a long time by the reform community, especially groups like Common Cause, Public Citizen, and Public Campaign. The journalistic community has itself relied heavily on these groups, especially Common Cause, for much of its information on how the campaign finance system works, including making extensive use of the massive data collection and analysis done by Common Cause from Federal Election Commission raw data.

The political science community has done its own extensive research on campaigns and campaign financing, but for most of the post-1974 period, its work was largely ignored by reporters, interest groups, and politicians alike, especially when it contradicted their own assumptions and assertions. This despite the fact that much political science research has been constructive in identifying the real problems, looking at what is real and what is hyperbolic in the rhetoric about campaign finance and the political system, and examining realistic and reasonable ways to deal with real problems.

In 1996, I joined with some of my colleagues in an effort to change the campaign reform dynamic. I convened a small group, including political scientists/campaign finance scholars Tom Mann of the Brookings Institution, Michael Malbin of the State University of New York at Albany, and Tony Corrado of Colby College, and veteran journalist Paul Taylor, who was engaged in an effort to bring free television time to the political process. Lawyer and former chair of the Federal Election Commission Trevor Potter agreed to provide advice and counsel.

We discussed the then-prevailing dynamic in the political arena of the debate on campaign reform: Democrats insisting on comprehensive reform including spending limits and public financing; Republicans insisting that no reform could include spending limits or public funding. Democrats got kudos for their stance from reform groups and editorial writers; Republicans got kudos from their base voters and activist conservative groups and journals, and the result was impasse. We systematically discussed the real problems in the campaign system, including those that had emerged or grown with the 1996 campaign, and discussed what kinds of directed reforms could address those problems.

We outlined the prevailing philosophy of many longtime reformers, especially on the left, that money in politics was itself evil and should be reduced as much as possible, including by lowering the existing individual contribution limit of $1,000, which had been unchanged since its enactment in the mid-1970s. We saw a system where demand for resources had increased regularly and substantially while supply had been sharply restrained—leading to corruption and massive efforts to evade the rules.

We critiqued the emerging viewpoint of many conservatives that all campaign limits should be removed, with disclosure and the marketplace acting as the regulatory regime. We saw the result not as the equivalent of a free economic market, but as the equivalent of "frontier capitalism": a market system where there is no parallel to the Securities and Exchange Commission; no required annual reports; unlimited insider trading; no penalties if powerful regulators coerce investors to put their money into stocks the regulators prefer. Moreover, the disclosure advocated by Rep. John Doolittle (R-CA) and Tom DeLay (R-TX), the aptly named major conservative advocates of this approach, explicitly excluded any disclosure for the electioneering communications conducted under the guise of issue advocacy, thereby creating a giant loophole that would render disclosure virtually meaningless.

Our group discussed several realistic goals of meaningful campaign reform. *First*, reform should lower the barriers of entry into politics that campaign costs have created; fewer and fewer people without independent wealth have been able or willing to take on the money chase that is inevitable in today's congressional campaigns. *Second*, reform should reduce the obsession that all candidates—including incumbent lawmakers—have with raising money, which diverts their time and energy from things like lawmaking. *Third*, reform should reduce the relative role of interested money, and enhance the role of small givers who have no direct and immediate interest in legislation—in the process giving more citizens a stake in the political process. *Fourth*, reform should retain as much of the market system—where candidates have to go out and compete for funds, showing a broad base of citizen support—as possible. *Fifth,* reform must allow enough resources for campaigns to be robust sources of dialogue and deliberation, educating voters through their give-and-take. It is very expensive to get any message, commercial, political, or otherwise, out to people in a large society bombarded with a cacophony of information 24 hours a day.

The result of our discussions and deliberations was a targeted reform agenda, which turned into a report entitled "Five Practical Ideas for Campaign Reform." Our plan was endorsed by the League of Women Voters. The idea of focusing on specific incremental reforms was embraced by Senators McCain and Feingold for the revised version of their signature campaign reform bill, as was our idea for dealing with the sharp rise in electioneering advertising by outside groups in the guise of "issue advocacy."

Our approach to soft money, focusing on abolishing federal soft money and prohibiting transfers among and between state parties and national parties, and creating separate overall individual contribution limits for candidates and parties, was adopted by a group of congressional freshmen led by Democrat Tom Allen of Maine and Republican Asa Hutchinson of Arkansas.

After a vigorous public debate about the efficacy and constitutionality of identifying "sham" issue advocacy as communications mentioning the name of a candidate within 60 days of the election, we reconvened our group, added University of Virginia Law School Professor Dan Ortiz and Brennan Center Executive Director Joshua Rosenkranz, and engaged in a vigorous dialogue about how to revise our original plan. We drafted a new proposal that focused on electronic communications, over a threshold dollar amount, targeting candidates close to an election. Our proposal banned money from union dues or corporate coffers for those communications and devised a disclosure scheme for larger individual donors for such ads.

After campaign reform legislation failed in the Senate in part over the question of "paycheck protection" for labor union members, Senator Olympia Snowe of Maine sought a new, bipartisan approach to deal with this problem. She embraced our idea; working with a bipartisan group of senators, she moved it into legislative language as the Snowe/Jeffords Amendment, offered it on the floor of the Senate when campaign reform was debated in 1998, and saw it adopted with 52 votes. It, of course, went down with the rest of reform on yet another Senate filibuster.

Campaign reform has emerged anew in 2001, with Senators John McCain and Russell Reingold bringing a new version of reform, incorporating Snowe/Jeffords, up early in the 107th Congress, creating a new opportunity for compromise. The opening for targeted, incremental reform has clearly been influenced considerably this time by the work of the scholarly community, bringing theoretical, practical, pragmatic, and political considerations to bear.

Realistically, reform will not occur with a mere 60 votes in the Senate overcoming the intense opposition of Republican leaders like Trent Lott and Mitch McConnell. It will come with a compromise hammered out by reform advocates and leaders of both parties. A compromise, of course, could be a disaster—one designed to appease everybody that strips down reform to a couple of basics, ignoring loopholes and creating unintended consequences. But a truly constructive reform with wide bipartisan support is in fact possible. What would it look like? It would have many of the following elements:

1. **Ending soft money—the right way.** For any opponent of complicated regulatory regimes, soft money should go. It was a creature of a regulatory body, a separate source of money for "party-building," that has been systematically distorted and misused by both parties. There should be one kind of money in politics, with no artificial distinctions in how the dollars can be used. The trick is to make sure that there is enough hard money available for the parties to accrue for their activities. An appropriate compromise would be to end soft money at the federal level; end any transfers from one state party to another, or from a state party to the national; ban federal officials, including the president and vice president, from soliciting or raising state party soft money.

   In addition, a compromise would create a separate limit on the hard money individuals can give to the parties, and make it reasonably generous—say, $30,000 per year, indexed to inflation; there would also be a limit of $30,000 per cycle for individual contributions to candidates. Currently, individuals can give a grand total of $25,000 per year to candidates and parties, with a sublimit under that of $20,000 to parties. That leaves little opportunity for the political parties to raise hard money—hence, they have turned even more to the soft variety. Creating a separate and generous limit for parties would solve that problem, while removing the worst abuses on the soft money side. It would eliminate the corruption that comes with unlimited contributions, especially the shakedown of donors by powerful politicians, and make everybody more honest.

2. **Tackling the phony "issue ad" problem by barring unions and corporations from electioneering.** George W. Bush's own reform proposal called
   for eliminating corporate and labor soft money, with leaving individuals
   alone. That reflected an understanding that corporations and unions are different. This is a distinction both Congress and the Supreme Court themselves have made often. Congress banned direct corporate contributions for
   campaigns in 1907, and for labor unions in 1948. The Court has upheld
   those bans numerous times. Beginning with 1994, unions, especially, began
   the use of massive ad campaigns disguised as "issue advocacy," with little
   issue content but lots of targeted attacks on lawmakers they want defeated.
   They can use union dues (as corporations can use money directly from their
   coffers) as long as their ads don't use the so-called "magic words" defined
   in a footnote in the Supreme Court's *Buckley v. Valeo* decision as express
   advocacy—words like "vote for," "vote against," "elect," or "defeat." Political science research led by David Magleby of Brigham Young University
   has shown that this Court standard is, at minimum, obsolete—only *four* percent of candidate ads in 2000 used such magic words! For ads of this sort
   run right before the election, clearly designed to elect or defeat candidates,
   union dues and corporate funds should be banned, leaving that right to individuals.

3. **Disclosing the funders of electioneering ads.** The First Amendment
   clearly grants individuals the right to run issue communications. But voters
   have the right to know who is communicating. Many of those using the
   guise of issue advocacy to electioneer have deliberately gone out of their
   way to disguise their identities; for example, the Wylys, who masterminded
   the attack ads run by "Republicans for Clean Air" against John McCain's
   environmental record, had a right to fund the ads. But in major part because
   of their friendship with George W. Bush, they went out of their way to disguise their identity, going so far as to pay two intermediaries to keep their
   role hidden. Major investigative work by reporters identified them, but few
   of these massive last-minute attack campaigns, especially if they target a
   congressman or senator, will be given the same scrutiny by dozens of top
   reporters. Broadcast ads attacking candidates should have their true sponsors and patrons disclosed—not just some sham front person. Broadcasters
   are required to record the sponsors of genuine campaign ads they air; they
   should have a similar requirement for electioneering ads, but one that gets
   behind the façade—and they should put the identities of the sponsors on the
   Internet for all voters to see and assess.

4. **Making robust disclosure the answer to the "paycheck protection"
   problem.** A key stumbling block to a broad bipartisan resolution of the
   campaign reform problem has been the Republican leadership insistence on
   "paycheck protection"—the right of union members to veto in advance the
   use of any of their dues money for purposes they do not like. Unions, like

corporations (and Congress, for that matter) are representative institutions, with elected leaders who are given discretion to use their revenues. As a citizen, taxpayer, and voter, I can't veto the use of my tax dollars for pork barrel projects; all I can do is vote for representatives who share my values, by assessing how they vote.

The best way to hold elected leaders in representative institutions accountable for how they use the dues (or taxes) paid by those who they represent is to have full disclosure of how the money is spent. Currently, corporations do not have to disclose in their annual reports any of their political spending, including soft money, and unions do not have to disclose how they spend their dues moneys in politics, including the so-called "issue advocacy" campaigns against congressional candidates or get-out-the-vote efforts. The answer to the call for paycheck protection is to pass Snowe/Jeffords (see numbers 2 and 3, above) and to include a provision for real disclosure—then let union members who don't like how their money is being spent vote for new leaders.

5. **Raising the contribution limits for individuals.** The drive for campaign finance reform from the left has been animated by a deep-seated conviction that the process is corrupt, with well-heeled donors buying influence, and votes, from lawmakers. A massive amount of research has failed to find any relationship here. The money chase is corrupting in many ways, including the possibility of buying and selling votes and the reality of buying access, and the reverse corruption of those with the power of the state using that power to coerce contributions from wealthy donors and institutions in a kind of "shakedown." That calls for eliminating soft money, where unlimited contributions remove any protection for potential donors. But limits on individual donations are a different matter.

    The need of candidates to raise adequate monies to get messages across in a cacophonous society has been frustrated by low limits, leading to much of the subterfuge that has taken over the campaign system, and encouraging the proliferation of multimillionaire candidates. At minimum, individual contributions to candidates should be raised to take into account inflation over the past quarter century, raising them from $1,000 to $3,000, and they should now be indexed for future inflation to avoid the same problem a decade and more from now.

6. **Getting small donors back into the political system.** Some elements of the Left may be mistaken about current contribution limits, but they are absolutely right that the field should not be dominated by the biggest donors. The last 15 years has seen a precipitous decline in the proportion of small donors involved in political giving at the federal level—mostly dating from the time that the Tax Reform Act of 1986 eliminated the tax credit for small political contributions. It is time to bring it back—this time as a 100 percent credit for contributions of $100 or less, with the credit limited to lower- and

middle-income people. That would keep the cost down and avoid giving a windfall to large donors. Many states have their own tax credits for small donors—they work, bringing more people into the game and giving them a stake in the political system.

7. **Creating a "seed money" mechanism to make it easier for nonwealthy candidates to get a campaign started.** More needs to be done to reduce the barriers to entry for potential candidates for federal office. Here is one way: Early in a campaign, let candidates for federal office raise up to $100,000 in contributions of up to $10,000—all immediately disclosed on the Internet and in the press. This would give potential candidates a chance to test the waters, form an organization, get rolling, and lower considerably the many "barriers to entry" candidates now face.

8. **Leveling the playing field for nonmillionaire candidates.** The First Amendment clearly protects individuals spending their own money in their own campaigns. No reform can change that. But reforms *can* make it possible for nonmillionaires to compete. How? Raise the contribution levels for candidates faced with opponents spending tons of their own money. If a candidate's opponent spends $100,000 of his or her own money, let the nonwealthy candidate raise up to that amount in contributions of up to, say $5,000—and let that candidate do so for each $100,000 a self-financed candidate spends. This will make it easier for nonmillionaire candidates to run and may discourage millionaire candidates from spending their own funds in an attempt to win by the sheer muscle of their own money.

These reform ideas focus both on restricting some of the abuses that have expanded in the past few election cycles, and expanding the resources available to candidates to enhance competition and campaign dialogue, and to broaden the field of potential candidates. There are two additional steps that are a part of the plan my colleagues and I have set out. One is to create an effective enforcement mechanism for campaign finance laws, by reforming and streamlining the Federal Election Commission. The second is to expand the resources available to parties and candidates, by creating a broadcast bank, filled with minutes of broadcast advertising time, distributed to parties (as a partial substitute for soft money) and to candidates as matching incentives for raising small individual contributions.

Over the past five years, the dynamic surrounding the debate on campaign finance reform has changed. So, too, have the prospects for campaign finance reform. Something might happen—and it might well be both real and constructive.

About the Contributors

Stephen Ansolabehere is Professor of Political Science at MIT and coauthor of *The Media Game* and of *Going Negative*.

Alan Gerber is Professor of Political Science at Yale University and author of numerous articles focusing on American elections.

Ray La Raja is Assistant Professor of Political Science at the University of Massachusetts Amherst and a Citizens' Research Foundation scholar. His recently completed doctoral dissertation is on political parties and soft money.

Gerald C. Lubenow joined *Newsweek Magazine* in 1965 as a correspondent in Atlanta and was named San Francisco Bureau Chief in 1969. After leaving *Newsweek* to serve as Assistant Executive Editor of *The San Francisco Chronicle* in 1984, Lubenow returned to *Newsweek* and was named London Bureau Chief. In 1990, he left *Newsweek* to become Director of Publications at the Institute of Governmental Studies at the University of California, Berkeley. Since 1999, he has also served as Director of the Citizens' Research Foundation, a campus-based campaign finance research institute. Lubenow edits the *Public Affairs Report,* a quarterly newsletter on politics and public affairs, and is the editor of a three-volume series on the California governor's race and a text on California government.

Kenneth R. Mayer is Professor of Political Science at the University of Wisconsin-Madison. He has written extensively on campaign finance reform, authoring *Public Financing and Electoral Competition in Minnesota and Wisconsin*; *Issue Advocacy in Wisconsin—Analysis of the 1998 Elections and a Proposal for Enhanced Disclosure,* and *Campaign Finance Reform in the State.* In 1997, he served as a consultant to the State of Wisconsin, Governor's Blue Ribbon Commission on Campaign Finance Reform.

William G. Mayer is Associate Professor of Political Science at Northeastern University in Boston. He has published books and articles on a number of topics, including public opinion, presidential elections, media and politics, political parties, and the presidential nomination process.

Robert E. Mutch, now an independent scholar (New York University Ph.D.), has taught at Rutgers, Barnard, and Brooklyn colleges and at the George Washington University. He is the author of *Campaigns, Congress, and Courts* (1988), a political history of federal campaign finance law since 1907, and of several articles on campaign funding practices and regulations.

Norman J. Ornstein is a resident scholar at the American Enterprise Institute for Public Policy Research. He serves as an election analyst for CBS News, writes regularly for *USA Today* as a member of its Board of Contributors, and writes a column called "Congress Inside Out" for *Roll Call* newspaper. In 1997–98, he was cochair of the President's Advisory Committee on the Public Interest Obligations of Digital Television Broadcasters. He currently leads a coalition of scholars and others in a major effort to reform campaign finance and codirects the Transition to Governing Project, an effort to create a better climate for governing in the era of the permanent campaign.

E. Joshua Rosenkranz is the founding president and CEO of the Brennan Center for Justice at NYU School of Law, where he has litigated, drafted legislation, and written extensively on issues of democracy, primarily campaign finance reform. He is the author of *Buckley Stops Here: Loosening the Judicial Stranglehold on Campaign Finance Reform* and *Voter Choice 1996: A 50-State Survey of Ballot Access Rules.* He is co-author of the forthcoming *What Choice Do We Have?* and the editor of *If Buckley Fell.* His articles on campaign finance have appeared in the *New York Times,* the *Washington Post,* the *Boston Review,* the *Chicago Tribune,* the *American Prospect,* and *The Nation.*

James M. Snyder, Jr., is Professor of Economics and Political Science at MIT and author of numerous articles on electoral and legislative politics.

Clyde Wilcox is Professor of Government at Georgetown University. He has written a number of books, chapters, and articles on campaign finance, gender politics, religion and politics, and other topics. He is coauthor of *Serious Money: Fundraising and Contributing in Presidential Nomination Campaigns,* and is currently working on a book on contributors to congressional campaigns. Before entering academia he worked for the Federal Election Commission.